THIS IS A CARLTON BOOK

Design copyright © Carlton Publishing Group 2003. Text copyright © Ingrid Sommar 2003

This edition published in 2003 by Carlton Books Ltd. A Division of the Carlton Publishing Group, 20 Mortimer Street, London. W1T 3JW

All rights reserved. A CIP catalogue for this book is available from the British Library. ISBN 1 84222 631 2

Research: Emma Andersson, Community, Malmö
Executive Editor: Sarah Larter
Art Direction: Alison Tutton
Picture research: Stephen Behan, Stephen O'Kelly and Ingrid Sommar
Production: Marianna Wolf

scandinavian style

classic and modern Scandinavian design
and its influence on the world

ingrid sommar

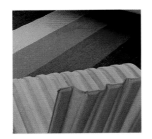

INTRODUCTION NATURE AND CULTURE

Looking at Scandinavian Style today, it appears at first glance to be a mid-twentieth century phenomenon. In 1947 furniture, glass, household articles and handicrafts from Sweden, Norway, Denmark and Finland had been displayed at the legendary Milan Trienniales – the ultimate showcases for modern design – where they made a dramatic impression. In the autumn of 1949, *Time* magazine featured a cover image of "The Chair" by the Danish furniture designer Hans J. Wegner, and devoted a considerable number of pages to the burgeoning Scandinavian design phenomenon. Over the next decade the designs and products of the five Nordic nations reached the height of fashion, and the influence of Scandinavian design grew worldwide. The style of the Scandinavians also became part of a much broader design style, and, in hindsight, the similarities between the work of international contemporaries such as Italian Gio Ponti, Americans Charles and Ray Eames and Dane Arne Jacobsen are apparent.

During the 1990s the ideas of that era were reinterpreted and resurrected by a dynamic new wave of designers. However, the origins of a particular "Scandinavian Style" can be traced much further back than the period immediately following the Second World War. To understand the durable simplicity that has developed in the north – characterized by clean lines, practicality, craftmanship and democratic ideals – you have to go back many centuries to the peasant societies that originally dominated the region and which made a powerful contribution in shaping the culture of the Nordic countries.

The customs of the rural population played a decisive role in laying the foundations for the practical and austere designs that increasingly influenced their surroundings. In mainland Europe the opposite was generally true and it was the ideals of the ruling class that governed. The Scandinavian view of design has been characterized by generations of farm workers and fishermen who constructed their own buildings, boats and furniture from materials that were close at hand. Wood from the forests, mainly pine and spruce, was the dominant raw material and has – in contrast to most other countries – continued to be one of the most important building materials in modern times. Granite, clay, leather and metals were other obvious materials used for houses, furnishings and household articles. Linen, wool, sheepskin and furs were utilized for clothing and for domestic textile requirements. The palette favoured by the inhabitants of the frozen north was light and pallid, the opposite end of the spectrum to the rich, deep tones of the Mediterranean countries.

The idea that even mass-produced goods should have an appealing and practical design was articulated in Scandinavia at the end of the nineteenth century, as was the belief that good products and homes should be available to all. By the beginning of the twentieth century, artists were being recruited by factories in Denmark, Sweden and Finland to contribute to the concept of beautiful everyday articles. As a result of these practices, Scandinavian glass, porcelain and silver attracted attention at the world exhibitions as far back as the 1920s.

At the end of that decade the Nordic countries, like many others throughout Europe, adopted the ideas of Modernism. The ethos behind this movement was that functionality is inherently beautiful, and that, when it comes to adornment, "less is more". It was a philosophy that the Scandinavians recognized, and that fitted their natural traditions like a glove. During the 1930s the first steps were also taken in several of the Nordic countries towards the modern welfare state. The edifying idea that good design was an obvious democratic right was soon to be found on the political agenda.

Names such as Gunnar Asplund, Alvar Aalto and Arne Jacobsen were to be found among the Modernist pioneers, others included Kaj Franck, Bruno Mathsson and Wegner. The work of these groundbreaking designers is still prominent, and has continued to be an inspiration for later generations. By the 1950s, when "Scandinavian Design" suddenly became an accepted concept throughout the world, these designers were still (with the exception of Asplund who died in 1940) at the height of their creativity. Jacobsen had just completed the Ant Chair, and was on the point of getting to grips with the more organically shaped Egg and Swan chairs and the furniture and fittings of the SAS Royal Hotel in the centre of Copenhagen, which has now achieved cult status. Inspired by nature, Aalto had designed the Finnish Institute of Technology in Helsinki, and progressed in his furniture designs from the radical bent-wood stools, chairs and armchairs of the 1930s and 1940s to equally consistent and functional lighting. Franck was hailed at the 1951 Milan Trienniale for the tableware he had created and, in 1955, produced another immortal glass vase that became a constant source of plagiarism, the waisted cylinder with a spout called "2744".

Scandinavian design continued to be popular in the decades that followed this golden era, mainly as a result of the efforts of the Danes and the Finns. Norwegian and Icelandic design had never been quite as influential, and the endeavours of Swedish designers to achieve the twin ideals of beauty and functionality became eroded – with the exception of glassware – by increasing consumerism and mass-market production.

Now that the spotlight is once again on Scandinavian design the central principles influencing it are in many ways brand new. During the 1990s a new generation of designers attempted to reinvigorate the somewhat tired concept of "Scandinavian Style", however, its essence is not easy to capture. For are there really any points of contact between, for example, the Finnish sculptor, architect and product designer Stefan Lindfors and the Swedish graphic designer Henrik Nygren? The former has a wild streak and an untameable lust for experimenting, creating useful household articles and dramatic interiors such as those for the Gershwin and Mercer hotels in New York. As the *Sunday Times* said in 1992: "To describe Stefan Lindfors … as an industrial designer would be like calling a complex Stravinsky symphony a nice song." Nygren on the other hand concentrates on detailed handicrafts, and is continually seeking simplicity, a philosophy that can be appreciated in the conceptual programme of the Baltic Art Centre, which opened in 2002 in Gateshead in the northeast of England. Is there really any correlation in their work other than that they are both Scandinavians, designers and working internationally?

The answer is both yes and no. It is not a homogeneous idiom that unites today's Scandinavians and that – possibly – provides them with a distinguishable style. What, on the other hand, they have in common is closeness to an unusually wild and beautiful landscape and roots in the simple, economic and useful design culture of the Nordic heritage. Both are sources of inspiration with rich veins that have shown themselves to be remarkably tenacious.

NORDIC HERITAGE: THE MODERN VERSION

With its timeless, temple-like crematorium building Woodland Cemetery in Stockholm, which was designed by the Swedish architect **GUNNAR ASPLUND** (1885–1940), has had a documented impact on twentieth-century Modernism worldwide. Built in the late 1930s, the cemetery's organic whole, including its surrounding, masterfully balanced grounds, has been listed as a Unesco World Heritage site since the 1990s.

The huge black letters dominating the graphic identity of the Baltic Art Centre in Gateshead, England, which opened in 2002, are both strong and utterly simple. The two Swedes who created the graphics for the Baltic, **HENRIK NYGREN** and **GREGER ULF NILSSON**, clearly belong in a contemporary world. However, the visual impact of their work also evokes the early industrial roots of the former mill, which has been transformed into an contemporary arts centre.

NORDIC HERITAGE: THE ANCIENT VERSION

The stone church in Jelling, Denmark was built between the tenth and twelfth centuries, and is characteristic of the architecture of the Middle Ages in northern Europe. Simple values, an austere appearance and laborious carpentry marked the Nordic building tradition even then. With its ancient burial mounds and traditional runestones, Jelling's church has been listed as a World Heritage Site.

The expressive textures and patterns by Danish textile designer **VIBEKE ROHLAND** have often been displayed in prestigious global contexts such as the *International Design Yearbook*. Exquisite textiles spring from her imagination and span wide ranges, from screen-printed cottons with names like "Abstract Archaeology", to *crepe de chines* with pop-sounding labels like "Juicy Lucy".

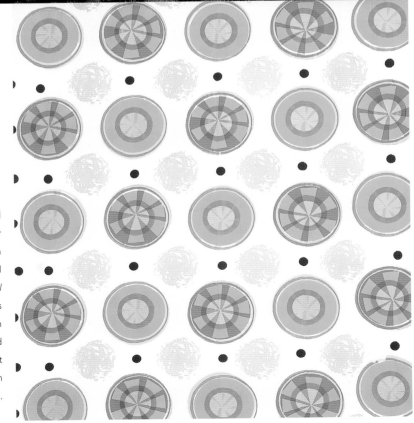

NORDIC HERITAGE:
THE GUSTAVIAN VERSION

Snow falls heavily and tough winds blow on the Finnish fort of Sveaborg, which is situated on an isolated island in the Baltic archipelago outside Helsinki. Originally aimed at defending the then Swedish–Finnish empire from the Russians, it is today used as a Nordic arts centre. The fort's buildings and interiors are also fine reminders of eighteenth-century Gustavian style. Simple and functional, yet graceful and elaborate, the style was a direct result of King Gustav's intense interest in French and Italian culture.

Finnish designers – including **STEFAN LINDFORS** (born 1962) today and **ALVAR AALTO** (1898–1976) in his time – have often been influenced by their native environment with its raw climate and fresh, beautiful nature. At the same time they have dared to explore the outside world, challenged by new techniques and futuristic visions. This is a typically uncompromising salad bowl and cutlery designed by Lindfors.

East and west, north and south – they all meet in the façades of Egypt's new Alexandria library, which was designed by Norwegian architects **SNØHETTA**. Bridges, spanning history and culture, are built as monumental, geometric forms. Additional encyclopedic values are gathered on the engraved stone wall designed by Norwegian ceramic artist **JORUNN SANNEM**, which displays the letters of alphabets from all over the world.

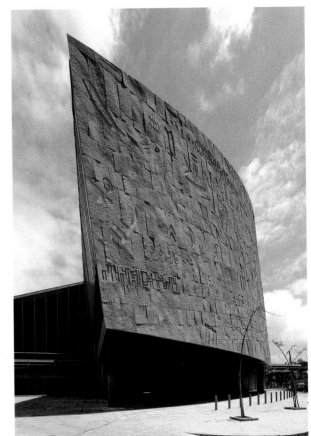

NORDIC HERITAGE:
THE FOLKLORISTIC VERSION

In Urne's stave church, which sits by Sogne Fjord in western Norway, and dates from the eleventh century, the richly decorated patterns of the shingled benches, walls and ceilings take on an almost baroque dimension. The building shows that in the popular culture of the Scandinavian countries, the wish to create beauty did not always lead to austerity. Like Jelling Church and Asplund's crematorium, the stave church by Sogne Fjord has been listed as a World Heritage Site.

Iceland's eerie volcanic landscape has stayed at the heart of Western culture since the birth of the Nordic Sagas many centuries ago. Today it still offers vital inspiration for new generations of Icelandic designers and architects, immersing themselves in both regional and global values.

"... thought I could organize freedom -– how Scandinavian of me" Iceland-born artist **BJÖRK** sings on her 1999 album *Homogenic*. The utterly sampled image of this unique artist – transcending genres, all kinds of boundaries and layers of time – still has a distinctly Nordic touch. Exotically Icelandic.

ARCHITECTURE ARCHITECTURE ARCHITECTURE ARCHITECTURE ARC

Functionalism was the name that Scandinavian architects gave to their interpretation of twentieth-century Modernism, although in the English-speaking world the preferred term was "International Style". The Nordic variant was more pragmatic, socially involved and, in terms of the actual designs, more restrained. It was an architecture directed at ordinary people and their wellbeing, creating quality of life rather than art, and complementing the philosophies of the Scandinavian welfare states.

As International Style developed, the world's architectural cognoscenti began to form its own image of Scandinavian architecture and design. Viewed from the outside, Scandinavian architecture became synonymous with the sum of the qualities of Gunnar Asplund, Alvar Aalto, Jørn Utzon and Sverre Fehn. It was perceived as an architecture borne of classically oriented humanism and Functionalism; inspired by nature, it was organic and thoroughly craftsmanlike. The Scandinavians themselves, meanwhile, saw it as a utilitarian architecture that worked for the good and use of all. Crucially, however, they perceived themselves as individual entities: Danes, Finns, Icelanders, Norwegians and Swedes – not representatives of a common Scandinavian ethos. From a Scandinavian perspective, the differences between the individual nations were greater than the similarities.

For a long time, Nils-Ole Lund, a professor of architecture who works in Denmark, Norway and Sweden, took the opposite view. In his book *Nordic Architecture* (1991) he emphasized the need for greater agreement between the five countries and argued that the common cultural identity should be explored. Lund expressed the belief that the architectural history of the Scandinavian countries was a mix of European and Nordic national history, stating that: " ...the major changes have been made on the European plane while the nuances can be seen in each and every one of the Nordic countries." He was also convinced that "interest for the region as a whole results in a partially altered view of architectural history in each country."

Scandinavian architects are now more in tune with his ideas. Elements of a common, Scandinavian architecture are apparent, even when viewed from within the individual nations. The *Nordische Botschaften* (Nordic embassies) in Berlin, which opened in 1999, are evidence of this. On a plot of ground near the leafy Tiergarten, enclosed by a ring of high copper sheets are the five Nordic embassies, together with a complementary *fælleshus* (meeting house) for joint activities and events. The five embassy buildings have been designed by architects from each of the countries, with the Austro-Finnish firm of architects Berger-Parkkinen responsible for the basic plan, the overall exterior design and the *fælleshus*. There is no doubt that there is a strong relationship between the buildings, all are austere, geometric structures that have been given warmth and sensuality through the careful use of natural materials, primarily stone and wood. *Nordische Botschaften* has become one of the major architectural sights in Berlin and is both a contemporary update and reflection of modern Scandinavian architectural traditions.

Similar things can be said of the number of ambitious terminal and airport buildings that have recently been constructed in various parts of Scandinavia. An increasing degree of construction throughout the world is dedicated to supporting global travel, not least by air. Much like the medieval cathedral, the international airport is becoming one of the most overrated and competitive architectural commissions, in which architects fight to create the most sensational and futuristic monuments to global travel. This is as true in Scandinavia as it is in the rest of the world, where a number of new buildings have been constructed, including an exceptional flight control tower in Sweden that was designed by Gerd Wingårdh. Here traditional modern Nordic ideals have been fused with more international architectural ideals with a distinctive result.

The era of traditional Scandinavian economy and moderation seems to be passing. A new generation of architects has made its presence felt increasingly since the middle of the 1990s, and is not afraid of expressing itself forcefully and with powerful gestures. These architects move gregariously on the international stage and succeed in conveying sophistication and the extremes of architectural drama.

In Sweden it is primarily Wingårdh who has led the movement towards a bolder expression. In Denmark, a country where architecture has steadily progressed internationally since the days of Arne Jacobsen, firms such as Schmidt, Hammer & Lassen, 3 x Nielsen and Vandkunsten have continued to develop the country's architectural profile. Other Danish architects such as Dissing & Weitling, Knud Holscher and Henning Larsen have worked on international projects such as the Kunstsammlung (art collection) Nordrhein-Wesftalen in Düsseldorf or the exotic Foreign Office in Riyadh, both of which were approached with Nordic consistency and quality. A number of Finnish firms such as Heikkinen-Komonen, Arrak and Artto-Palo-Rossi-Tikka have been also given the chance to set a fresh imprint on major, prestigious buildings internationally. In Norway Snøhetta has risen as a major name on the world stage at the same time as other, younger firms such as Jarmund & Vigsnæs have distinguished themselves. Among Icelandic architectural firms it is mainly Studio Granda that has been responsible for instilling innovative ideas into important projects.

At the same time the Nordic architectural foundations have shown themselves able to integrate and match the pace of shifting international values. Time after time architects from geographically remote Scandinavia have won competitions for culturally and conceptually complicated buildings on far away continents. At the end of the 1950s, when interest for Scandinavian Style was still at its peak, the Dane

Jørn Utzon won first prize in the competition to design Sydney Opera House. It was erected during the following decade and has since achieved a position as one of the world's most famous and iconic constructions. Forty years later the Norwegian firm Snøhetta repeated the feat, this time for a new library in Alexandria, Egypt, which was built during the 1990s and opened in 2002.

In Utzon's case it was a pronounced organic architectural view that ensured that his distinctive and expressive ideas could easily be transferred from one cultural sphere to another. In the case of Snøhetta and the Alexandria library it is more about a profound humanism that has been capable of cutting through time and ideas. The library building is supported by a stark structure that has the ability to awaken a spectrum of disparate associations. When the international architectural and design magazine *Domus* wrote about the building, it stated that "the exterior of the library suggests a charming allusion to the symbol of the ancient sun god Ra" while "the hypostyle organization of the reading rooms is cognate with the great mosques of North Africa". But there are also more well-known Nordic elements such as the "soft wooden surfaces, the acid-stained bronze panelling and the benign glow of filtered light that contribute to a resounding sense of serenity". For the library's magnificent southern façade, clad in granite, Norwegian artist Jorunn Sannem created a pattern in the form of letters. Incorporated in this jumble of symbols from all the world's alphabets it is possible for thousand-year-old Norse runes and Egyptian hieroglyphics to join together naturally on the same surface.

The architecture of Swede **GUNNAR ASPLUND**, who is often seen as the father of Scandinavian Modernism, lingered between the neoclassical ideals of the 1920s and pure Functionalism – the Scandinavian interpretation of twentieth-century International Style. The neoclassical inspiration is clearly evident in the Woodland Chapel, Stockholm, which was built between 1918 and 1920, and was partly influenced by an idyllic rural mansion on the Danish island of Moen.

The Austrian architect **JOSEF FRANK** (1885–1967), who moved to Sweden in the 1930s from Adolf Loos's Vienna, contributed to the early years of Modernism in the Nordic countries. He was particularly influential with his simple summer houses in Falsterbo, southern Sweden, including Villa Carlsten (above, 1927), which helped pave the way for new building ideals. Frank later abandoned Functionalism, developing instead a personal, comfortable, organic style, and concentrating successfully on interiors, furniture and textiles.

In Finland the Functionalist era was dominated by the strong, creative personality of **ALVAR AALTO**. From the start of his career his influential Modernist interpretations had a clear organic touch, which is clearly shown in the sanatorium building at Paimio (right, 1929–33). It was while working on this building (see also opposite, bottom) that he started experimenting with the bent plywood furniture that was later so closely associated with his name.

In the groundbreaking, Villa Mairea (1939), which was built for the rich Gullichsen family, Aalto excelled in unconventional uses of his favourite material – wood, particularly Finnish birch and pine. Commentators have described Aalto's handling of the wooden sources as original, but never implied eccentricity. He worked with a "quality of inevitability derived from his craftsmanlike pleasure in perfecting the design".

Between the 1920s and the 1970s Aalto's architecture transformed from being symbolic of a rational new era, to becoming an expression of the past. However, the ability to master an organic whole shows both in the early buildings such as the Paimio Sanatorium (right and opposite top), and in later works, including the Finlandia building (above, completed 1975). Housing a concert hall and congress centre, and situated close the shore of the Baltic Sea, the Finlandia building is now an established Helsinki landmark. The white façades, which were constructed from plaster in Aalto's buildings of the 1920s, were fashioned from marble 50 years later, linking Finnish culture to Mediterranean tradition.

The Nordic Embassies in Berlin, which were designed by prominent middle generation architects from each of the five nations, form an unusual manifestation of contemporary Scandinavian Style. Wrapped in a common façade, designed by Finnish–Austrian architects **ALFRED BERGER** and **TIINA PARKKINEN**, the five free-standing embassies share a common square. The Norwegian Embassy (opposite) was designed by **SNØHETTA**; the Danish Embassy (above left) by **3X NIELSEN**; the Finnish Embassy (above centre) by **VIIVA**; the Icelandic Embassy (above right) by architect **PALMAR KRISTMUNDSSON**; and the Swedish Embassy (right) by **GERT WINGÅRDH**.

Next to Gothenburg's Liseberg amusement park lies Wingårdh's Universeum Science Center (above), the building itself is an integral part of the educational project, producing its own energy and containing advanced systems for recycling water and waste. Inside the building visitors can walk through natural biotopes and eco-systems, following water from mountain waterfalls to salt-water aquariums. The building, which was inspired by a traditional barn and is divided in four parts, is covered with a vast and idiosyncratic roof.

Two of Swedish architect **GERT WINGÅRDH**'s recent public buildings. The impressive black-and-white striped control tower (opposite) stands at Arlanda airport, outside Stockholm. Composed of two circles, one black and one white, the shaft's contrasting stripes are decorated with quotations from French writer Antoine Saint-Exupéry's "Postal Right South", an idea of the Finnish artist **SILJA RANTANEN** and much appreciated by the architect.

The Danes dominated Scandinavian architecture towards the end of the twentieth century. The most renowned personality, is the Danish architect **HENNING LARSEN**, who has worked frequently abroad with a *genius loci*-sensitive version of traditional Modernism. He has also designed many contemporary buildings in Copenhagen, including the Unibank offices (above).

The pharmacy in Taastrup (left), designed by Danish architect **KIM UTZON**, pays evident respect to the admired Scandinavian architectural tradition.

"The Black Diamond", the new National Library in Copenhagen, was designed by Danish architects **SCHMIDT, HAMMER & LASSEN**, and has aroused admiration and debate. With its glass and limestone façades overlooking the water in Copenhagen's old harbour area, the building is part of a grand harbour renovation scheme. Part of the interior decoration is a large ceiling painting by artist Per Kirkeby.

In a short time Icelandic architects **STUDIO GRANDA** have succeeded in designing a great number of internationally noted public buildings in their home country. Their portfolio includes a Supreme Court, an Art Museum (above) and Reykjavik City Hall (right). A building split in two, the lighter office building of the City Hall, predominantly fashioned from glass, seems to stand directly in the lake.

Danish architect **KIM UTZON**'s own house near Helsingør uses a simple wooden structure. Inspiration came from organically developed villages in locations all over the world. The load-bearing construction is based on wooden telephone poles.

Transparency is one of the dominant themes in the Architect's Building in Copenhagen, designed by Danish architects **3 X NIELSEN**.
Wooden screening on the inside of the façades subdues the otherwise strict impression of glass and steel.

In the construction of the FIH commerce bank, also designed by **3 X NIELSEN**, transparency is key. The architecture of the FIH building, which is situated right at the Copenhagen harbour front, refers to Dahlerups Pakhus, an old, preserved warehouse nearby. However, the new bank building is light and cut through with multi-storey gardens.

Danish architect **SØREN ROBERT LUND'S** Arken Museum of Modern Art on the Ishøj coast south of Copenhagen is reminiscent of a ship wrecked on the shore. Unlike most of his Danish colleagues, Lund favours expressive formal gestures. The museum's outstretched building has its centre in a curved "art axis", from which sculptural forms and deconstructed elements reach out into the landscape.

In the Trädgårdsföreningen restaurant and cultural centre in Gothenburg (opposite) Swedish architects **STUDIO GRÖN** wanted to transform memories of the actual building site by rooting concepts of modernity within innovative, contemporary forms.

Neomodernist approaches can be seen in the work of many young Scandinavians. Danish architectural duo **ENTASIS** want to "give form to the Utopian vision of classic modern man". Their entrance building for the Zoological gardens, Copenhagen (above and left) utilizes elements such as dynamic open spaces and columnar structures with the ambition of melding impressions of the past with vital ideas about the future.

Finnish architects **ARTO PALO ROSSI TIKKA** like to treat their buildings as if they were miniature cities. The Sibelius Congress and Concert Hall in Lahti (above) stands on the site of a former factory. Behind the vast glazed façade the interior is constructed from different kinds of Finnish woods, celebrating the nation's traditional craftsmanship and showing different structures and metaphorical themes for the building's various functions.

The Finnish embassy in Washington DC, designed by architects **HEIKKINEN-KOMONEN**, resembles a simple cube. The east and west façades are green granite, the veins of the stone intertwining with the branches of the surrounding trees, while the north and south façades are constructed of translucent materials such as glass and glass blocks.

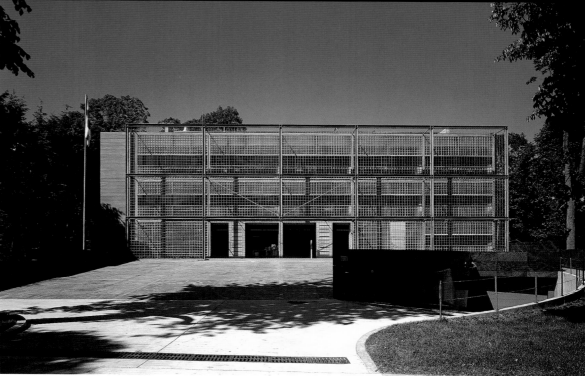

Karmøy Fishing Museum on Norway's rocky west coast represents the area's long standing seafaring and fishing culture. Norwegian architects **SNØHETTA** designed a sculptural museum building, delicately placed within the landscape. The result was reminiscent of the simple structures of the local fishing industry, yet articulated in a unique contemporary manner.

The dramatic arctic landscape plays an evident part in some recent pieces of Nordic architecture. Norwegian architects **JARMUND/VIGSNÆS** use the spectacular natural surroundings of Spitsbergen as a challenge for the architecture of the Governor's headquarter in Svalbard (above). The angled walls increase the floor area, without the need for more pillars, which would have been difficult to anchor in the frozen ground.

Another exotic architectural creation from the far north: the Glacier Museum and research centre in Fjærland, which adorns western Norway's steep landscape of fjords. It was designed in the 1990s by **SVERRE FEHN** (born 1924), the doyen of Norwegian architecture.

The Icelanders built a health and tourist centre right in the middle of a volcanic landscape. In the Blue Lagoon, which was designed by Icelandic architects **VINNUSTOFA**, wooden bridges take the spa guests over the natural hot springs, while exterior screening shields from harsh winter storms.

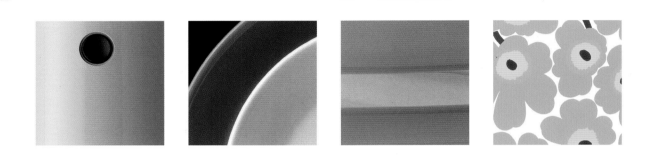

Harmony and beauty were the elements with which Scandinavian design was fundamentally associated with in the 1950s. This was particularly apparent in the realm of homeware, which together with furniture formed the heart of the concept of Scandinavian Style – resulting in pleasing, unexaggerated designs that conveyed a particular lifestyle. This style was inherent in all aspects of homeware – the elegant ceramics, serving dishes and spice jars; the unobtrusive, textured and naturally coloured "architectural textiles" that complemented modern Scandinavian furniture; the psychedelic, deep-pile rugs and fabrics; the sleek cutlery fashioned from stainless steel or silver; the imaginative, organic glass designs; and the rich production of beautiful and practical dinner services with both spare and more elaborate decoration. All these items contributed to the image of Scandinavians living a contented, civilized life, experiencing a culture for all, that was in a continual state of development.

Homeware in Scandinavia is still characterized by practicality and simplicity. But the beautiful utensils radiate an air of coolness that can exist anywhere in the world. Take as examples the shiny professional-style saucepans and cocktail equipment in stainless steel that are among some of the most praised of current Nordic design; the original dinner services, often monotone and extremely spare, but with distinctive individual details that turn the concept upside down; the smart plastic devices with a touch of avant-garde spice in the design that almost succeed in spiriting away the fact that these are low-cost items. These ranges convey a sense of cosmopolitan city life that is hardly reminiscent of the traditional, twee picture of the Nordic welfare state.

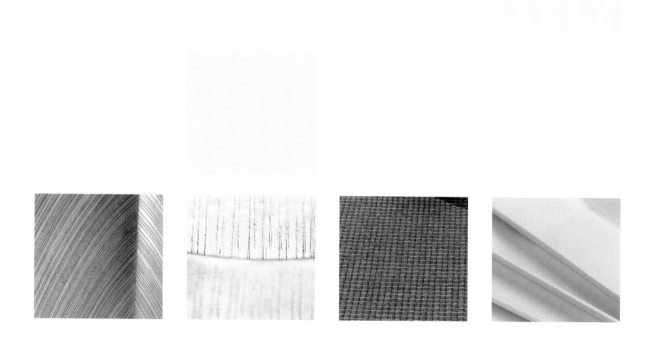

The coolness itself is a characteristic that is often given when it comes to today's Scandinavian design. "Refreshing as an iceberg" was the comment of the British designer Jasper Morrison on 1999's New Scandinavia exhibition – a characteristic that could also describe his own work. Suddenly the coolest continent's geographical situation with its snowy expanses and arctic cold has become as exotic and attractive as the sandy beaches and swaying palms of a South Pacific island.

Typical of northern design's new awakening is that contemporary designers are imbued with an international outlook from the outset. Furthermore it has become almost a given that Scandinavian designers succeed abroad only then to be discovered by the media and clients at home. This was certainly the case with the group of Swedish architects, textile and glass designers who were involved with the Italian firm Cappellini at the beginning of the 1990s. They were responsible for the production of a successful line of homeware called *Progetto Oggetto* long before they were known to the Swedish public. It was also the case with the Finnish design company Snowcrash, which created a buzz in Milan in 1997 before becoming all the rage in Finland. Meanwhile, the young design group Norway Says aimed its work directly and consciously at the international arena before choosing its somewhat cheeky name.

Even Scandinavian manufacturers have become more international in their outlook. So much so that practically all the old Nordic art industries that were at the forefront of the Scandinavian design revolution are today encompassed by two large multinational design groups – the Finnish company Hackman, which

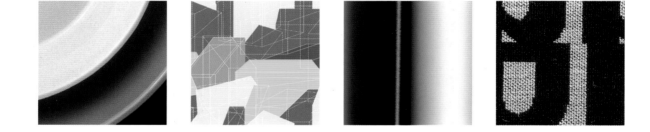

acquired the bulk of the Swedish chinaware industry, and Danish–Swedish Royal Scandinavia. Apart from its own brand name, which is responsible for homeware in materials from stainless steel to plastic, Hackman encompasses Finnish Arabia (chinaware) and Iittala (glass), Rörstrand (the Swedish china manufacturer) and parts of Gustavsberg. Royal Scandinavia includes the Danish china factory Royal Copenhagen, glassmakers Holmegaard and silversmiths Georg Jensen, plus the majority of Swedish glassmaking led by the Orrefors and Kosta Boda, glass, chinaware and cutlery from Swedish Höganäs and Boda Nova.

It was in these industries, the majority of which were founded in the eighteenth and nineteenth centuries, that the Scandinavian model took root in terms of design. At the beginning of the nineteenth century the companies realized that they had to modernize their production. This took place on a broad front by binding painters, sculptors, graphic artists and architects to the factories — who then themselves carved out individual roles as designers over the ensuing decades. They learned to work together with the company managers, technicians, foremen and workers to promote their practical and technical requirements, thus participating as equals in the industrial team. It was also typical of the Nordic model that the same companies – including those mentioned above and many others that have since closed down – produced both exclusive artistic products and mass-produced, carefully designed everyday goods.

The national design organizations have also played a decisive role in this development, even those that are more than a century old are still going strong. The oldest is Svensk Form (founded 1845), followed by Dansk Design Centre, Norsk Form, Design Forum Finland and Form Iceland. These organizations were inspired by art theorists such as John Ruskin and William Morris and also the Deutsche Werkbund, and aimed to foster good, democratic and practical design. Today the Nordic national design organizations

support and develop further design, not least by contributing to global marketing of each individual nation's innovations. The Dansk Design Centre has been especially successful in this respect.

At the beginning of the new millennium Scandinavian design has, however, started to become less involved with large scale, everyday products and increasingly with more exclusive items – despite the fact that the politically loaded slogan "beauty for all" is zealously used by the commercially successful mega-player Ikea. In reality, this development had already begun when Scandinavia was in the international spotlight in the 1950s. In his book *Scandinavian Design* (1961), the Swedish design critic Ulf Hård af Segerstad discussed the common design culture of the four Nordic countries (Iceland was not included at this time). He stated that the beautiful everyday products were still "of basic importance", although this was no longer the only guiding principle. In his opinion the steadily increasing production of practical articles must have a "sound direction" according to "the programme of the good article for everyday use". At the same time there was space for more expensive, unique items that could give "added value to our daily surroundings".

It is here that the old artisanal industries have taken up the baton to meet the demand for products that have inherent artistic workmanship and durability. Mass production of a high quality is today's Nordic recipe. The designers themselves seek more modern words for the new objects. One young Finn has talked about "nomadic artefacts for the lost urbanite", an unusually precise description of the twenty-first century's cool, cosmopolitan homeware from the hip but peripheral Scandinavia.

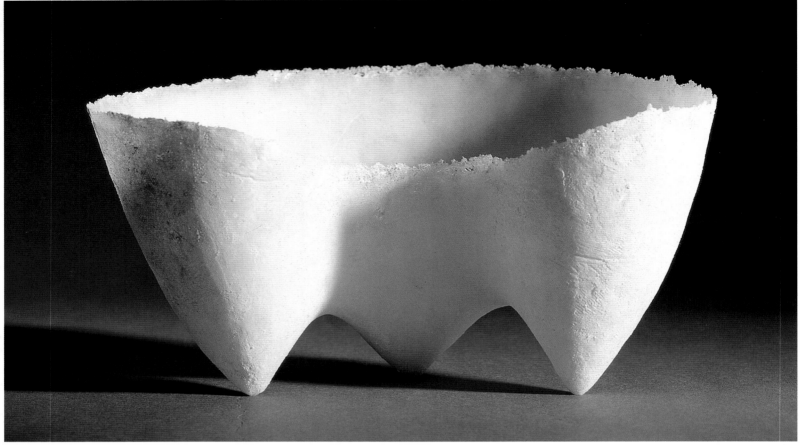

The inhabitants of the Scandinavian countries have always lived close to nature, which has had a strong impact on their lives and culture. This bowl by Finnish glass designer **PÄIVI KEKÄLÄINEN** is fashioned from *pâte de verre* – glass paste – a term that refers to objects made by fusing fine, often coloured fragments of glass in a mould. There are several different methods, and the final results can be either thick, solid, cast pieces or very thin shell-like objects, which are multicolored or white. Kekäläinen's delicate piece resembles ice.

One of the most solid Scandinavian classics is **ALVAR AALTO'S** Savoy vase (1936). The utterly simple, unique and fluid shapes of this vase, which is made in different sizes and proportions, evoke fresh, cool, running water. The vase also gives the flowers placed within it the appearance of irregularity and freedom. The Savoy vase is still in tune with times, remaining one of the icons of modern glass design. It is still produced by the Finnish company Iittala

Nature's materials, as well as the grandness and beauty of the natural environment, have been great sources of inspiration for the Scandinavians. With Finnish designer **TAPIO WIRKKALA**'s (1915–85) birch plywood bowl it is not difficult to see where his influences came from. What is significant about the natural shapes and forms of Wirkkala's work is that they always blended with urban environments perfectly. This leaf-shaped bowl was designed in 1951, and admired at that year's Milan Triennale; it was also named "Most Beautiful Object of the Year" by the US magazine *House Beautiful*.

The organic influences on Scandinavian design can be seen in the deep knowledge and skilled crafting of simple materials such as birch or pine, iron, stone, linen and leather. It is also evident in use of visual motifs, which originate in the dark green woods, blue lakes and white, snow-covered mountains of the Nordic landscape. The results of these influences can be seen in classic designs that are more than fifty years old, such as the wooden bowl below left, or in objects designed in recent last decades, such as the glass vases in the middle and to the right.

The simple teak bowl (above left) was designed in 1949 by Danish furniture designer and architect **FINN JUHL** (1912–89) together with Danish industrial designer and silversmith **KAY BOJESEN** (1886–1958).

The contrasting styles of contemporary Swedish designer **PER B SUNDBERG** can be seen in the simple glass vases titled Earth (centre). More forceful and brutal are the sculptural shapes Sundberg used in the massive Move vase for Orrefors.

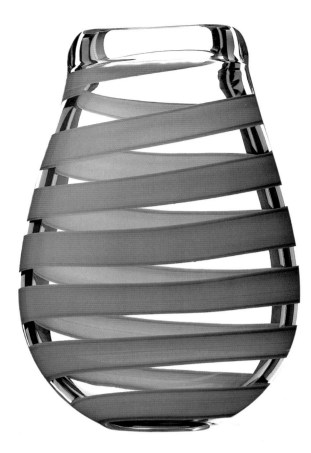

The Swedish designer **ANNE WÅHLSTRÖM** (born 1956) joined glass manufacturer Kosta Boda in the 1980s, before which she trained in textiles and in the American studio glass movement. Together with **GUNNEL SAHLIN** (see p. 73) she brought new vitality to the world of Swedish glass. Wåhlström's strong, colourful, organic shapes for her vases and bowls take their themes from the atmosphere and the ocean, with names such as Cyclone (above), Clouds (below), Orca and Seadragon.

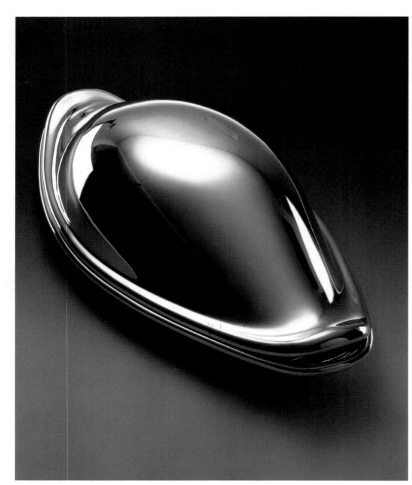

Renowned Danish silversmith
HENNING KOPPEL
(1918–81) brought a new
simplicity to the noble art
of shaping this precious
metal in the years following
the Second World War. His
fish platter for Georg Jensen
(1954) is seen as one of the
highlights of Danish silver
design of the twentieth
century. The dish is
beautifully simple and
harmonious, as natural in its
shape as if it were itself a fish
to be placed on the table.
The silver dish is made
by hand and it demands
up to 500 hours of work.

TAPIO WIRKKALA was Finland's most productive designer in the years following the Second World War and his Ultima Thule set of glasses (1968) were an important contribution to the international breakthrough of Finnish glass manufacturer Iittala. Wirkkala's Italian friend, the architect and designer Gio Ponti, used to call the Finn a "child of nature", and the obvious references to ice and cold in the design of the Ultima Thule glasses has ensured that these distinctive classics of the 1960s are still in production today.

Another Finnish classic, which is more admired and popular than ever, is Finnish textile designer **MAIJA ISOLA**'s (1927–2001) Unikko floral pattern (opposite). Designed in 1964 it has had a huge revival decades after its conception and, at the beginning of the new millennium, it is regarded as something of a Marimekko trademark. A recognized force in contemporary textile design, Maija Isola's work has been shown in numerous exhibitions all over the world, and acknowledged with many awards.

Paper yarn is a genuinely natural material made from a renewable natural resource that is produced ecologically – wood. Finnish textile artist **RITVA PUOTILA** has rediscovered this material and the traditional technique of producing it, imbuing the method with an aesthetic refinement and strength. After coming to international notice in the early 1990s with a collection that originally contained just paper cord rugs, Woodnotes, which is the name of the Puotila family business, has expanded to produce window blinds, bags and upholstery fabrics. The felt slippers shown in the bottom image were designed by **PIA WALLÉN** (see p.161).

One of the most important aspects of Scandinavian design, from its heyday in the 1950s until today, is the democratic vision – the outlook of "beauty for everybody". With his stainless steel cutlery, Danish industrial designer and silversmith **KAY BOJESEN** created stylish everyday tools that are found in many Scandinavian homes (right).

Designed in 1932, the pressed drinking glasses created by Finnish designer **AINO MARSIO AALTO** (1894–1949) were originally named Bölgeblick. Renamed Aalto and slightly re-shaped, the glassware went back into production for Iittala in the early 1990s. However, the general impression of the glass drinking set, which won Aino Aalto (who was the wife of Alvar Aalto) the gold medal at the 1936 Milan Triennale, remains.

The fight within the Scandinavian nations for higher quality in the industrial production of everyday goods and "beauty for everybody" was exemplified by the Finnish designer **KAJ FRANCK** (1911–89). He played a vital role as artistic director at porcelain and glass manufacturers Arabia, Iittala and Nuutajärvi during the decades following the Second World War. Among many other beautiful and useful household goods Franck designed the timeless Teema tableware (1977), which is still thought of as revolutionary, functional, and durable. Despite its classic status, it is everyday tableware in many Finnish households and it is still produced today.

Swedish textile designers **SALDO** intend their textile patterns to include elements that tickle the imagination – whether cheerful or serious, exciting or annoying. Their designs are often expressions of everyday activities and structures that are not obvious fields of inspiration for a decorative pattern. The pattern at the top is entitled Bullitt after the movie starring Steve McQueen; below that is a textile design entitled Network, which is intended to depict random yet interconnecting events; bottom left is entitled Poison 2; and bottom right is Urban: Lago Agrio, which is part of a series of five textiles, each based on the "colours" of a world city, in this case in Ecuador.

"... for everybody" also means designs that function for the elderly and disabled. Pioneers in this field of industrial design have been the **ERGONOMI DESIGN GROUP**, which was established in the late 1960s and is one of Sweden's biggest contemporary design studios. Among the group's international successes are tools for Bahco and ballpoint pens for those who suffer from rheumatism and arthritis. From top to bottom: in-flight serving dishes for Scandinavian Airlines, knives with ergonomic handles for Ikea and the Ideal kitchen knife for those with weak arms.

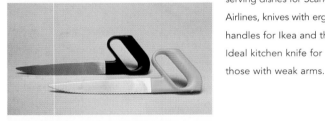

A covered trolley by **TIMO SARPANEVA** (born 1926), who is one of Finnish design's prominent international figures and is known for his skills within many design fields.

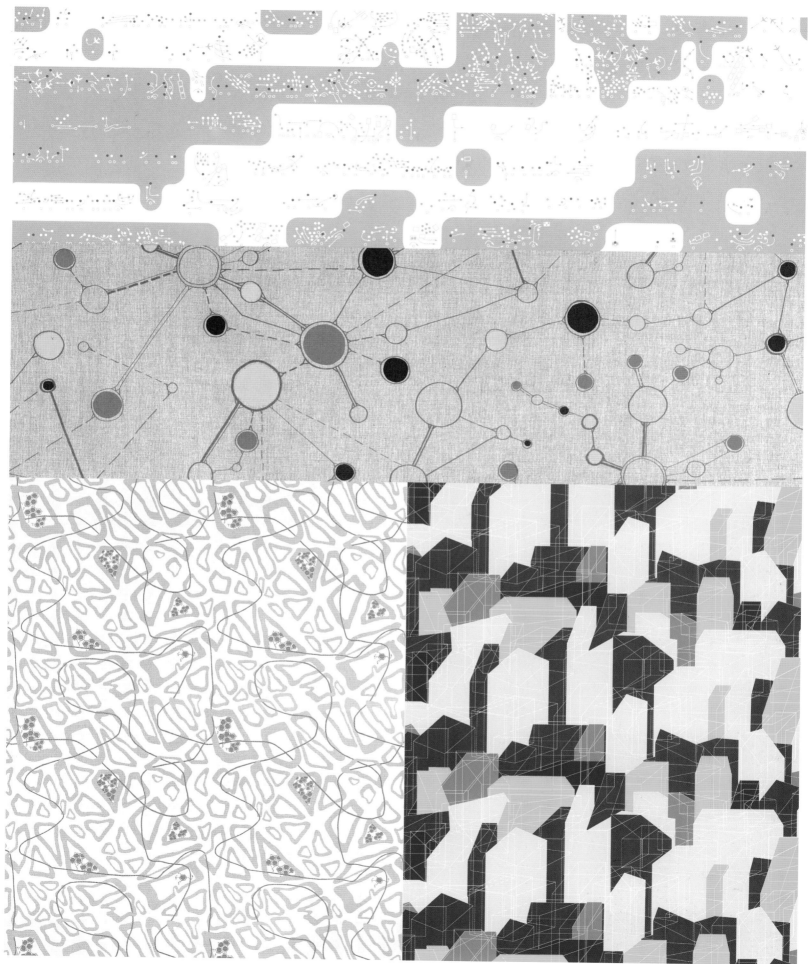

A Danish everyday classic: designer **GRETHE MEYER**'s (born 1918) Blue Line service has been among the most popular dinnerware in her native country since it was originally designed in 1965 for Royal Copenhagen. For the millennium Meyer updated the design, adding a palette of colours to represent each season.

Swedish interior architect and designer **ULLA CHRISTIANSSON** works with furniture and interiors as well as with tableware design. Her set of Globe drinking glasses for Design House in Stockholm follow simple curves and are reminiscent of the Scandinavian classics of the 1950s.

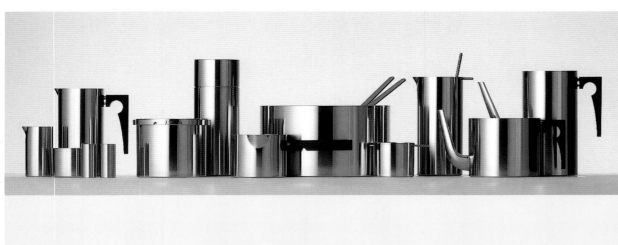

Modernism recycled: the stainless steel Cylinda Line series, which was designed by **ARNE JACOBSEN** in 1967, and was originally designed for the SAS Royal Hotel in Copenhagen (see p. 20), represents one of the broadest and commercially most successful applications of the functional principles for home consumption.

In 1977 Jacobsen's successor **ERIK MAGNUSSEN** (born 1940) designed a vacuum flask for Stelton. Intended to complement the classic Cylinda Line, it was a bestseller right from the start. Trained as a ceramicist, Erik Magnussen designs glass, metalware, cutlery and furniture. He reduces the variety and forms of his designs to essentials, making them interchangeable and stackable. The vacuum jug is manufactured in both stainless steel and coloured plastic, and the line has been extended to include sugar bowls and creamers.

The Eva Trio series of modern kitchen tools, which were designed by Dane **OLE PALSBY** (born 1935), were launched in the late 1970s, and thirty years later reached cult status among both amateur and professional chefs. The series, originally named Trio because of the three materials – steel, aluminium and copper – used in the saucepans (below), has grown considerably, today comprising all manner of cooking tools, including salad servers (left) and an ample collection of glass and steel lids (right).

The success of the strictly functional, Modernist Eva Trio line inspired the manufacturers to embark on a contrasting adventure in the late 1990s, the Eva Solo series. Here Danish designers **CLAUS JENSEN** (born 1966) and **HENRIK HOLBAEK** (born 1960) have had the opportunity to excel in softer and more decorative expressions. The glass oil and vinegar carafes (right) are blown by mouth and have pouring lips in stainless steel and silicon rubber, ensuring drip-free handling.

Scandinavian masters: **BERNADOTTE & BJÖRN**.

When Scandinavian design first became widely famous in the 1950s, the Nordic countries were also noted for their socially conscious welfare states. Newly built homes, supplied with all the necessary modern household goods and machines, implying a rising standard of living, played a vital role in this image. Founded in Copenhagen in 1950, Bernadotte & Björn helped to visualize this political progress. Swedish designer **SIGVARD BERNADOTTE** (1907–2002) and Danish architect **ACTON BJÖRN** (1910–92) created the largest and busiest industrial design studio in northern Europe. The firm's range encompassed interiors; furnishing components, such as patterned linoleum; technical products, such as office machines and radios; and homeware designs such as glass and cutlery. This set of knives, spoons and forks, was designed for SAS in 1966.

Modern everyday serving goods:
the Norwegian interpretation.
Porcelain manufacturer Figgjo's
Front series of serving plates were
designed by **JENS OLAV
HETLAND** and **OLAV JOA**,
and follow classic Scandinavian
themes. In production from 2000,
this award-winning series aims
at innovation and flexibility.
Each product can stand on
its own, or function with items
from other Figgjo lines.

Textiles always played an important role in the Scandinavian home. With their roots in simple natural materials such as linen and wool, the textile traditions of the Nordic countries have grown more urbane and refined, in terms of production techniques as well as patterns. Danish artist **GUNNAR AAGAARD ANDERSEN** designed this textile named Letters for Kvadrat.

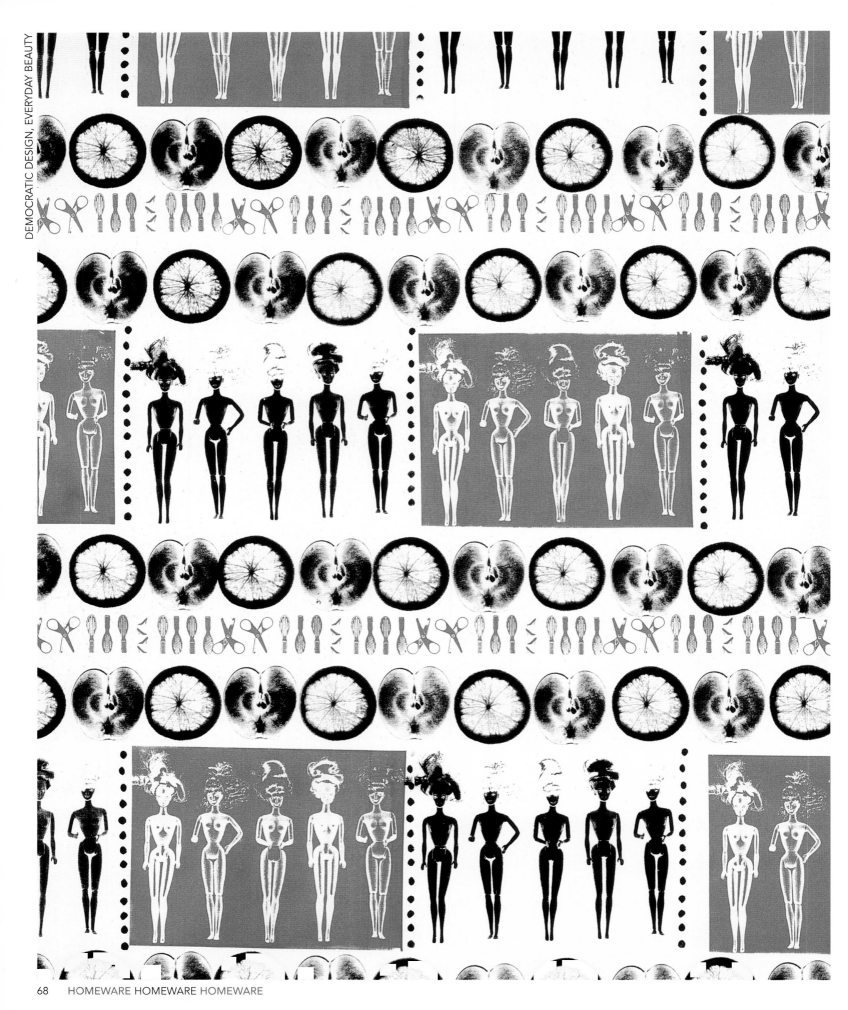

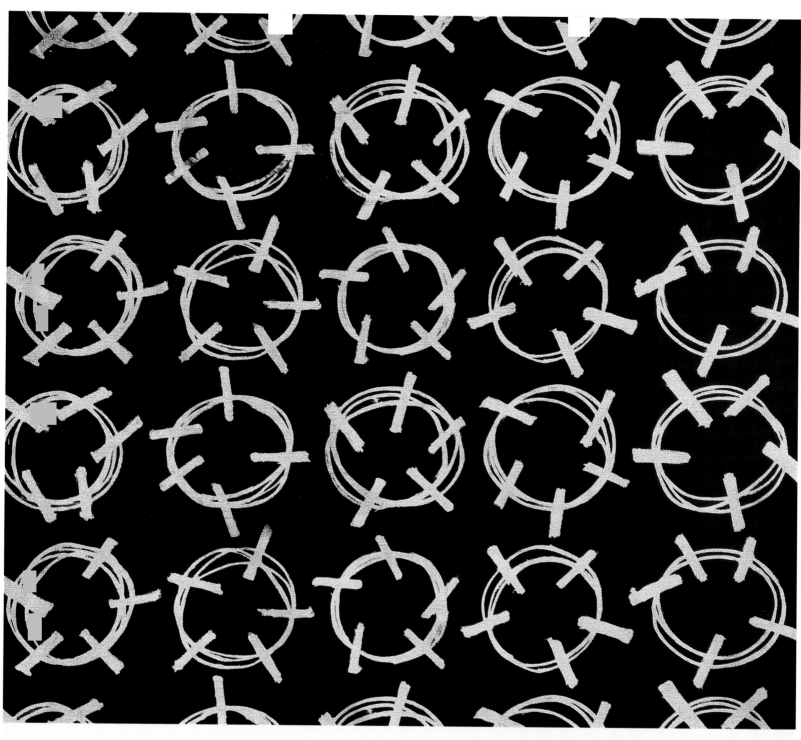

More innovative textile designs: Barbie is OK (opposite) and Bomulp (this page), both by Danish designer **VIBEKE ROHLAND**.

Simplicity always is a striking feature of Scandinavian design. The unconventional cutlery designed in stainless steel by Danish architect **ARNE JACOBSEN** for the SAS Royal Hotel in Copenhagen (1961) is a prime example. From the tiny coffee spoon to the long salad servers, all share flat, rudimentary handles that continue to the end of the utensils. Perfect for eating peas, but not as good for pasta, according to Italian writer Umberto Eco, who in an essay on "anonymous design" considered peas typically Danish food.

The Swedish silversmith and industrial designer **SIGURD PERSSON** (born 1914) designed this range of cutlery called Jet-line (1959). Fashioned from stainless steel, it won an inter-Scandinavian competition for the ideal set of cabin cutlery for use onboard SAS's new jet aircraft. The long handles and continuous lines are treated in a strong and personal way, yet show affinities with Jacobsen's cutlery. The range is still in production for Georg Jensen.

You don't have to follow the old rules, seems to be the design message of this twenty-first century dinner service. Called Ego it was designed by **STEFAN LINDFORS** for Arabia. Pure, austere and clean are the adjectives that are often used to characterize the works of Nordic designers, even those as individual as Mr Lindfors, who is an artist of all-encompassing skill. Easy-to-hold, the Ego range is a distinct design, and intended to suit all kinds of food.

Forever austere, the Scandinavian design tradition grew out of the culture of the poor, not out of wealth and sophistication. From the start, simplicity was essential, and today it has matured to become a deeply rooted tradition, fitting in well with contemporary trends of international Minimalism. These bowls and vases for Kosta Boda are by Swedish glass designer **GUNNEL SAHLIN** (born 1954).

Referring to Finnish roots: the material may be glass, ceramics, wood or stainless steel – the Minimalist's attitude never seem far away in the work of the new Scandinavians. These tough barbecue utensils by Finnish designer **HARRI KOSKINEN** (born 1970) for Hackman, get straight to the point, elegantly combining functionality and simplicity.

Basic forms open up to new possibilities. Finnish designer **PEKKA HARNI**'s ABC dishes for Arabia come in two forms and three colours, and their potential for variation seems vast. The simple geometry of the designs creates space, form and character.

The unique features of the Ursula series, by Danish designer **URSULA MUNCH PEDERSON** for Royal Copenhagen, are the oval saucers and the prolonged, sharp, almost sculptural lines of the spouts. As with the ABC range above, a few pregnant shapes and carefully chosen colours create innumerable possibilities of variation.

Simplicity has always been a striking feature of Scandinavian design. Swedish glass designer **INGEGERD RÅMAN** (born 1943) has made simple, traditional forms her mark of excellence. The forms she creates are almost ritually basic and are always treated in a timeless, contemporary manner, including these Skyline vases and decanters for Orrefors

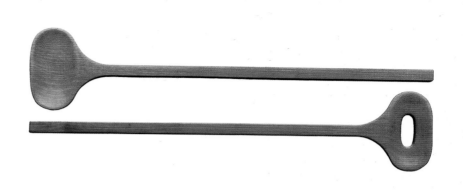

Scientific beauty. A collection of modern simple utensils unveiled by Hackman in 1998 has quickly become a range of veritable classics. Among the collection are Swedish designer **CARINA SETH ANDERSSON**'s salad bowls fashioned in two layers of matte-brushed stainless steel with a pocket of air between them, and her birch wood salad servers.

The old idea of a lantern transformed into cylindrical modernity. Finnish designer **HARRI KOSKINEN**'s lantern of clear or coloured glass stands on the border between being an everyday article and a sculpture. Still an utterly practical item, the lantern comes with a match holder to facilitate the lighting and snuffing of the candle.

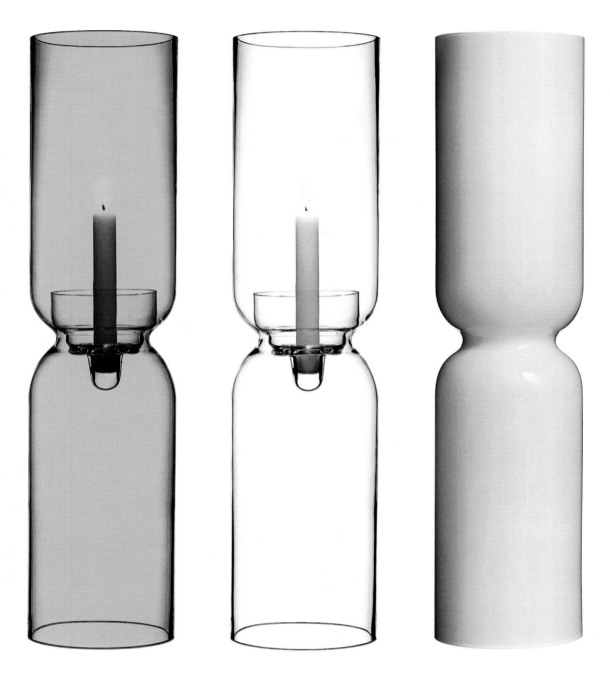

Links between Scandinavian and Japanese design have often been noted. In both cultures there are strong organic influences, and tendencies towards reduced expression. Japanese designer **FUJIWO ISHIMOTO**'s (born 1941) has worked with the Finnish textile company Marimekko for a long time. His highly personal work gave the company a boost during the 1970s and 1980s, with the styles more abstract than the playful designs that made Marimekko famous in the 1960s. Inspired by traditional Asian art and culture, and also by Finnish traditions and nature, Ishimoto has continued to reinvent himself.

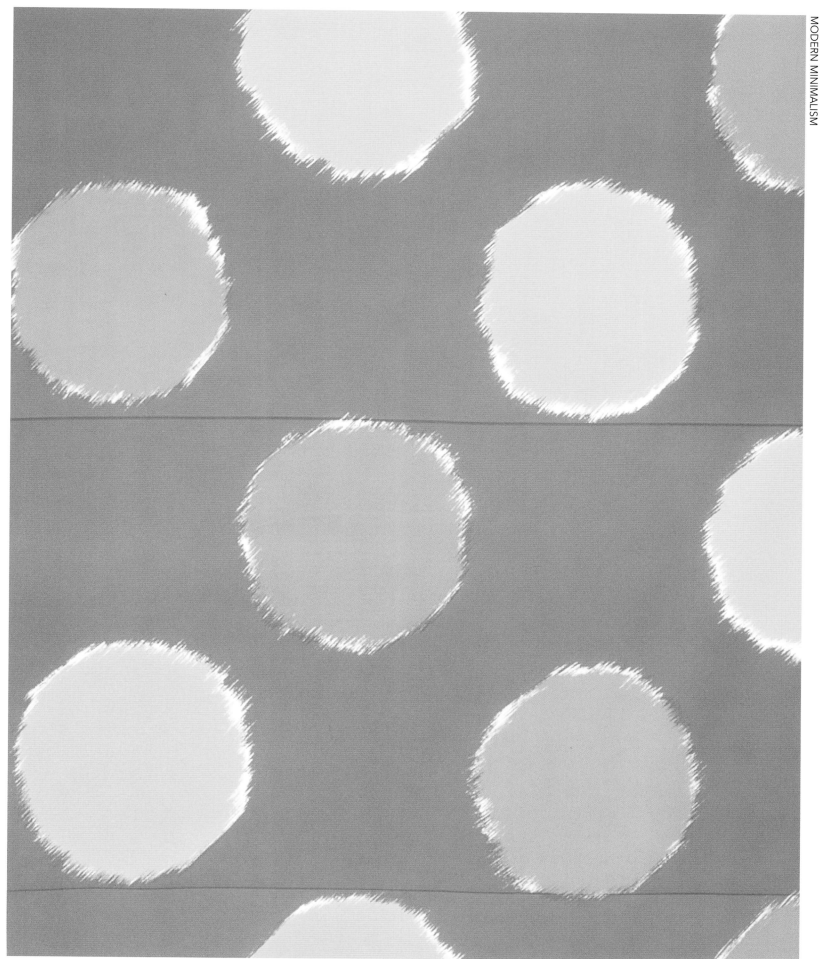

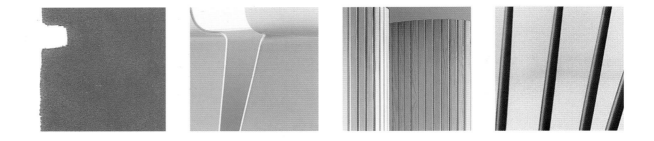

A strange event occurred prior to the opening of the Helsinki's Kiasma Art Museum in 1997. The elegant Triennale chair, which had been designed by the furniture professor Antti Nurmesniemi in 1960, suddenly went into production. The chair had been praised in the design press for decades, but until then had existed only as a prototype. The reason for its rebirth? Steven Holl, the American architect who had won the competition to design Kiasma, wanted the chair as part of the museum's fittings. A forty-year-old dream became reality, and it was now viable to start manufacturing this exclusive, clean-lined model of solid steel and leather. However, Holl's choice was not about nostalgia, quite the opposite; Nurmesniemi's unrealized masterpiece from 1960 is simply as relevant today as it was then.

This time-warp is typical in the creation of Scandinavian furniture today. Since the beginning of the 1980s a succession of Nordic designers have stormed onto the world stage with new, fresh, transparently international ideals. Above all a tendency to view furniture designs as individual, sculptured objects has developed. But even so, traditional Scandinavian values have shown themselves to be robust. The high morals of Nordic furniture creation during the 1930s and 1950s – detailed craftsmanship, impeccable functionality and the democratic involvement that lay behind all the persistent experimenting – still reap huge admiration internationally. At the same time it is becoming more difficult in today's trendy design shops to decide which of the attractive Scandinavian tables and chairs are half a century old and which have just been brought in brand new from the latest international furniture exhibition.

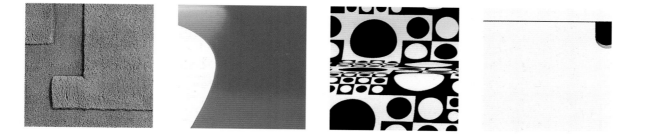

It is these undiminished furniture traditions that today's leading Scandinavian furniture designers – Finns Ilkka Suppanen and Timo Salli; Swedes Thomas Sandell, Claesson-Koivisto-Rune and Anna von Schewen; Tore Borgersen and Espen Voll of Norway Says; and Danes Kasper Salto and Hans Jakobsen Sandgren – can both revolt and rest against. Nordic giants have excelled in the majority of the most important styles that shaped twentieth-century furniture.

There is the modern wood tradition, which in itself covers several approaches. For a long time before functional ideas took root at the end of the 1920s, the Danes had a unique and well-developed tradition in carpentry, which was modernized by standard bearers such as Kaare Klint and Hans J. Wegner. What was important for them was not the creation of new models, but to the ability to obtain the best out of each material and its distinctive character. From this starting point the aim was to produce timeless, highly functional furniture. Designers were quite happy to model their work on international classics, for example on Chinese or British traditions, but they combined these influences with a precise sensibility for their materials and a carefully studied functionality that resulted in fresh, consistent design.

Meanwhile, in Finland, the country of the white-trunked birch, Alvar Aalto experimented from a quite different starting point. Early in the 1920s Aalto adopted the principles of Modernism and, in addition to his architecture, also become involved in the design of everyday articles. When it came to furniture, his intent was to replace the well-known experiments in tubular steel by pioneers such as Marcel Breuer and

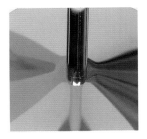

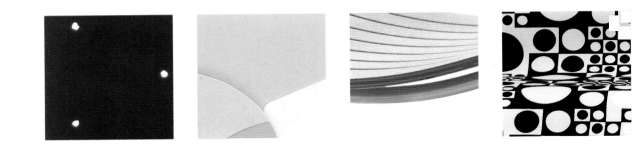

Mies van der Rohe with furniture made completely of wood, primarily using Finnish birch, both in the form of whole sheets and as laminated and bent plywood. These ambitions were realized and resulted in a growing collection of daringly designed stools, tables and armchairs all in the characteristic light blonde wood that seems just as contemporary today.

Danish designers, along with Breuer and van der Rohe, also played a leading role in the development of the modern tubular steel tradition. One of the most famous examples of this genre is the Ant Chair, which marked the beginning of Arne Jacobsen's efforts to bring together the harsh, industrial, tubular look of earlier decades with softer, more body-hugging designs. From this amiably shaped seat in shaped laminated wood he progressed to more organic designs, as is evident in the famous Swan and Egg armchairs. His starting point for these designs was the infinite number of types of foam and plastic materials that could be modelled and that technology now provided for designers. Design historians have entertainingly described how the functional Jacobsen, brought up to start with the material's distinctive character in the spirit of Kaare Klint, suffered agonies when confronted with flabby plastics with which you could do anything. The creative freedom seemed almost too great.

The limitless character of these modern materials was articulated in a striking manner by another Dane, Verner Panton, and his Panton Chair (1960). His designs appeared as though they had been "poured" or "kneaded" rather than built, and his methods inspired designers around the world. During the 1960s, the Scandinavians, along with the Italians, led developments when it came to ever increasingly colourful and imaginative shaped plastic furniture. In addition to Verner Panton, there were Finns such as Eero Arnio, Eliel Saarinen (who mainly worked in the USA together with designers such as Charles and Ray Eames) and Yrjö Kukkapuro. In the pop-

cultural spirit of the 1960s plastic furniture was given such rebellious names as "the pastille" or "the merry-go-round", names taken directly from low-cultural contexts such as sweet shops and fairgrounds.

The rebellious spirit still survives today. The Swedish starting shot in the Scandinavian design wave of the 1990s came with an armchair constructed entirely of cement with arms of rusty iron. It is hardly the most convenient or comfortable piece of furniture to have in your flat, but it is startling and stylish nonetheless. Such pieces are a clear reminder that design does not have to be deadly serious or take its inspiration solely from the traditional world of design – humour and a thirst for the genre are also required. The search for un-tested materials has recently been the most productive element among today's young Scandinavian designers. Unconventional furniture such as Flying Carpet, a beautiful armchair designed by Likka Suppanen that has a rug suspended on steel legs, and Anna von Schewen's Latta chairs, which are manufactured from braced and moulded material and sold by the metre, are good examples.

It could be thought that creating furniture has become more individual and is not as socially engaged as it was in the past. Just as in the world of fashion, trends come and go, but the links to society are still there if you look for them. For example, the need for meeting places is steadily increasing in the urban jungle of big cities. Today's designers are only too happy to work in smaller commercial arenas, those that exist for the good of all. In Scandinavia, libraries, cultural centres, airports, theatres, restaurants, museums and marketplaces have increasing importance as common spaces and inspiration for new furniture. The lounge, actually a semi-public intermediate zone, has become the darling room of the smart lifestyle magazines, where every piece of furniture has its real place, where the boundaries between the old, well-known functions are erased and the room resembles a landscape, full of as yet undiscovered opportunities and rigid ideas about function.

Swedish cabinet-maker **CARL MALMSTEN** (1888–1972) was a traditionalist, hating all things modern. A skilled craftsman, he wanted to explore cultural roots. His designs, like the Lilla Åland chair (below, 1940) are still effective, and the old Nordic simplicity in tune with modern times.

Another wooden classic. Finnish professor **ANTTI NURMESNIEMI** (born 1927) designed the emblematic sauna stool (below) as part of the interior of the Palace Hotel in Helsinki (1952). The design ideals were Functionalist, but the natural influences of Finnish nature and the traditional rite of the sauna have added timeless qualities.

Like the majority of Danish furniture designers during the twentieth century the master of them all **HANS J. WEGNER** (born 1914) has a background as a cabinet-maker. His speciality has been his ability to fuse traditional carpentry values with a variety of influences, from ancient China to English Windsor and International Style. His well-known Y-chair (above, 1950) is an interpretation of Chinese themes; it is still in production for Carl-Hansen & Son.

With its oatmeal-coloured webbed seat support, Swedish designer **BRUNO MATHSSON**'s (1907–88) bent-wood Eva chair (below, 1934) was a pioneering piece of Functionalist furniture. The elongated lounge chair shown here came a couple of years later. Lightness and elegance, as well as excellent function, were prime qualities in Mathsson's work. It is still in production for Dux.

Architects **THOMAS SANDELL** (born 1959) and **JONAS BOHLIN** (born 1953) designed the Snow series of cabinets as part of a furniture collection for Asplund that was manufactured in northern Sweden. The cabinets come in several sizes and proportions, with the carved, characteristic handles the only feature that is common to all models in the range.

Danish designer **PETER KARPF** first had the idea for the Nxt chair in the early 1960s. It took him thirty years to get the design produced, but the first chair was followed by an entire family of chairs, called the Voxia line. These include the Tri model (right) and the Oto lounge chair (opposite). What they all have in common are the basic production technique and common material -– moulded beech plywood, which has been bent in one piece without the use of a single screw or joint.

Swedish architect **JONAS LINDVALL** has been consciously trying to fuse today's international Minimalism with the crafted perfection of the Danish cabinet-maker's tradition. The S & B café chair produced by Skandiform is an example, as are the wooden pieces of furniture designed for the Koi sushi bar in Malmö (see pp. 1 and 129).

A controversial contemporary method of furniture construction has been the use of wood from old Swedish barns. The buyer of each piece receives full documentation on the building that was demolished, and from which the item was manufactured. **LEO THAFVELIN**'s rustic table for Arvesund is made of such aged, unique wood.

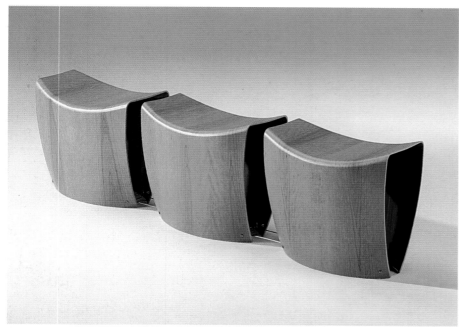

The bent-wood technique has a grand history in Scandinavia, with both Alvar Aalto and Bruno Mathsson among the international pioneers. The challenge to find new ways of using it is always there. Danish designer **HANS JAKOBSEN SANDGREN**'s Gallery stool, originally created for art exhibition rooms in Copenhagen, is moulded out of a rectangular piece of veneer.

This imposing chair by Swedish designer **MATS THESELIUS** for Arvesund is also made from material from an old barn. Theselius, however, chose somewhat provocatively to not to be nostalgic about the naked wood, instead he had his farmer's throne lacquered completely in blue.

A classic modern chair. A lot of attention has been given to proportion and detail in Swedish architect **JOHAN CELSING**'s Moses chair for Gärsnäs. The frame is solid beech, the seat and back fabric-covered beech plywood.

Internationally, architect **THOMAS SANDELL** is one of the most well-known contemporary Swedish designers. Sandell usually works with unexpected and innovative forms. His traditional Windsor chair for Allinwood is an exception, nevertheless the large horizontal back piece gives the chair a modern personality.

Immortal forerunners: **ALVAR AALTO**. In the early twenty-first century time has just caught up with the pioneering furniture designed in the 1930s by Finnish architect Alvar Aalto. Artek, the company founded by Aalto and his wife Aino in 1935, still produces the blonde Aalto classics in bent wood and birch, such as this 1935 umbrella stand in natural lacquered birch with a brass tray

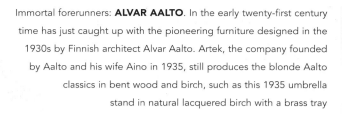

The organic language of Alvar Aalto's architecture is evident in the room-dividing screen (opposite, 1933), which uses vertically placed sticks in natural lacquered pine wood.

The revolution lay both in the daring forms, the bent-wood techniques and in the kind of lifestyle the new furniture signalled. Interiors were to be spacious and filled with light, therefore these were the perfect pieces of furniture to put in them. The birch armchair (left, 1932), is upholstered with one of Aalto's standard fabrics.

Webbing and quilted canvas were used a good deal for the early Scandinavian Modernist furniture, both by Aalto and Swedish designer Bruno Mathsson (see p. 82). The lounge chair (far left, 1936) came first; the small armchair with rattan or leather webbing (left, 1946) a decade later.

Immortal forerunners: **ARNE JACOBSEN**. It took Danish architect Arne Jacobsen years of intense experimentation to develop the Ant chair (1952) and the ensuing series of now classic, stackable, form-moulded chairs in laminated veneer with a tubular steel frame (left).

Innovative new foam materials became available in the late 1950s and paved the way for the Egg and Swan easy chairs (below, 1958) designed by Jacobsen for the SAS Royal Hotel in Copenhagen (see p.20).

Finnish designer **ANTII NURMESNIEMI**'s
elegant, functional and sculptural chair
Triennale 001 was first shown in Milan in
the early 1960s. When American architect
Steven Holl was looking for strong pieces
of furniture for the Kiasma Art Museum
in Helsinki, which he designed and
built in the 1990s, he rediscovered
Nurmesniemi's forty-year-old design
and chose it for the building. It is
now in production for Piiroiinen.

The variations on Jacobsen's original Ant concept – that, is the stackable and form-moulded chair on a tubular steel frame – are endless today, inside as well as outside the Nordic nations. With the Puma chair, manufactured by Källemo, Danish designers **BORIS BERLIN** and **POUL CHRISTIANSEN** of Komplot Design, have strongly emphasized the organic qualities of the piece.

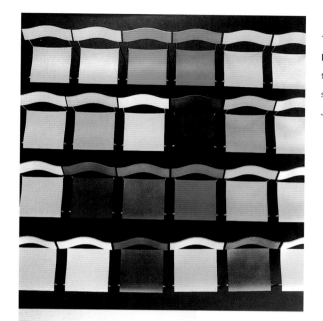

The Campus chair, designed for Lammhults by Danish architects **JOHANNES FOERSOM** and **PETER HJORT-LORENZEN** has a light back panel, which forms a wavy line when many chairs are standing together. The inspiration is clearly Arne Jacobsen's Ant Chair. In fact, it could refer to the undulating shapes of the chairs in the Bellevue Theatre, Klampenborg (see p.112), which was designed by Jacobsen in the 1930s.

The Clash stackable chair (left) by Finnish designer **SAMULI NAAMANKA**, which is manufactured by Martela, has treated the tubular frame in a different way to Jacobsen and most of his followers. The kinship is still there, though.

Swedish designer **MÅRTEN CLAESSON** of architects Claesson Koivisto Rune used a simple shape and a cut-out hole in the back, to make the Rodrigo 2 for Swedese stand out from other form-moulded stackable chairs.

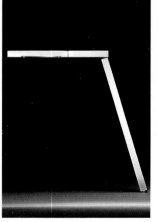

Danish architects **SCHMIDT HAMMER & LASSEN** developed the DKB reading lamps, while designing the building and interiors of the new National library in Copenhagen (see p. 31). The Minimalist design of the lamp bears a practical approach that is often comparable to the classic Danish PH-lamps of the 1930s: its shape ensures luminous efficiency, and it is adjustable according to the size of the table. The lamps are manufactured by Louis Poulsen.

Lightness is what Danish designer **KASPER SALTO** aimed for in his Runner chair for Fritz Hansen, the see-through construction imbues the piece with an airy impression. Admiring Modernist heroes such as Charles Eames, Arne Jacobsen and Mies van der Rohe, Salto has described the Runner chair as classic in looks, but modern in technical construction.

The Lamino armchair, designed by **YNGVE EKSTRÖM** (1956), is a much-loved Swedish classic that is still in production. In the first years of the twenty-first century the internationally successful Swedish trio of architects **MÅRTEN CLAESSON**, **EERO KOIVISTO** and **OLA RUNE** have acted as advisors for the manufacturers of Lamino, Swedese, building up an interesting contemporary furniture collection.

For Claesson Koivisto Rune global interaction in design is essential. In creating a more sophisticated design profile for Swedese they have collaborated with international designers such as Milan-based-Brit **JAMES IRVINE**. His Sonja chair shows great respect for Scandinavian Modernist roots.

Working on the Brasilia table **EERO KOIVISTO** faced a challenge that had earlier been met by Danish designer Peter Karpf (see p. 84). The elegant low table, which can also be placed bottom up, is constructed as one eternal loop, without joints or screws.

In their designs Claesson Koivisto Rune blend classic Scandinavian characteristics with cutting edge, contemporary international influences. The sumptuous Cloud sofa, designed by **MÅRTEN CLAESSON**, plays with traditional proportions and volumes.

Swedish designer **BJÖRN DAHLSTRÖM** (born 1957) started out as a graphic designer. Today he is based in industrial design, but he also works frequently with furniture. His BD1 chair, which is has been likened to a comma sign, has an innovative construction and a clearly graphic expression.

The stackable BD2 chair, also designed by Dahlström, differs from the general variations on the Jacobsen form-moulded theme in that it uses the sides of the seating shell as semi-armrests. The carefully formed and perforated sides add a visual signal, and at the same time heighten the chair's functionality. Both chairs are produced by CBI.

Former film-set dresser **GUNILLA ALLARD** (born 1957) is one of the most successful furniture designers in Sweden, working strictly in a Neomodernist manner. Her Cooper armchair for Lammhults owes a lot to pioneering Swedish designer Bruno Mathsson's Jetson chair, but still adds new qualities.

The mobile Tuesday armchair, designed by Swedish architect **LOVE ARBÉN** for Lammhults, indicates the influence of the early de Stijl constructivists, such as Gerrit Rietveld. Arbén's flexible little chair combines excellent practicality with a humorous and visually rich expression.

New practical attention given to old functional problems. Swedish architect **THOMAS ERIKSSON**'s (born 1959) combined mirror and towel rack for Asplund runs on wheels, and is easily transported.

The collection of innovative carpets, produced by Swedish company Asplund, has been frequently praised in prestigious contexts such as the *International Design Yearbook*.
Respected designers from all over the world have contributed to the collection. These three carpets are all hand tufted in 100 per cent wool and designed by Swedes. They
are: Cheese (top left) designed by **ANKI GNEIB**, Air (top right) designed by **THOMAS SANDELL** and JL , designed by **JONAS LINDVALL**.

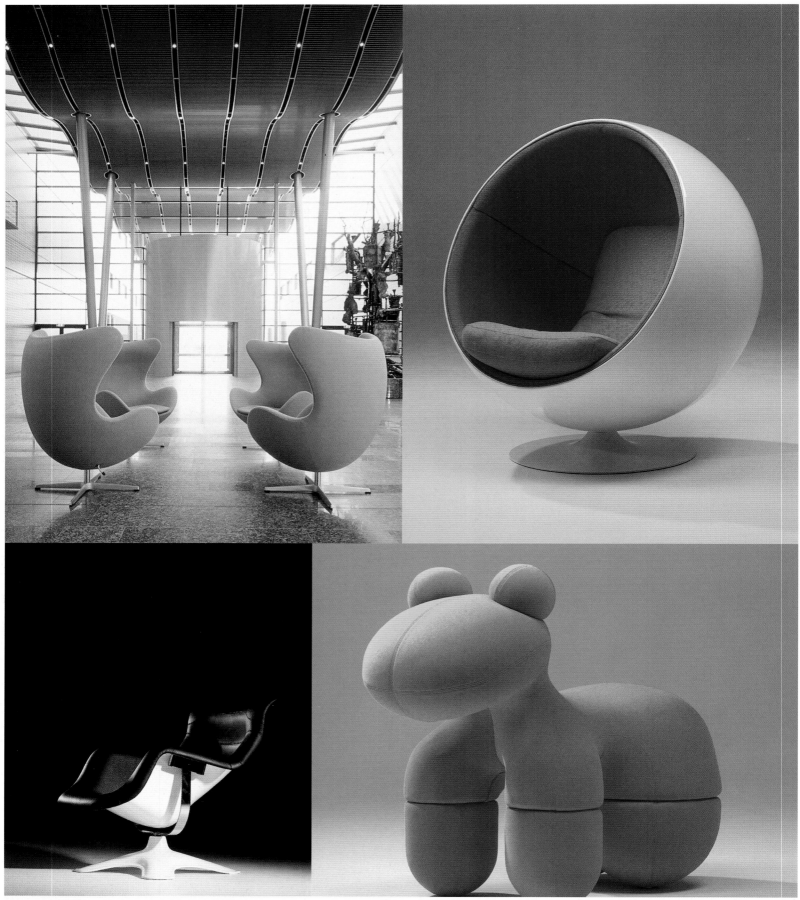

In addition to the emergent pop culture, the technical evolution after the Second World War nourished a liberated lexicon for furniture design. It wasn't as obvious any more that the shape of a chair was to show off first and foremost its construction. Instead revolutionary materials such as foam and plastic meant that a chair had the ability to look like just anything – an egg, a ball, a carousel or a pony. For Danish architect **ARNE JACOBSEN** it was a trauma leaving the safe old Functionalist ideal, and working without limits on designs such as the Egg chair (1958, opposite, top left).

Finnish designer **EERO AARNIO** (born 1932) belonged to the first pop generation, conquering the world during the Swinging Sixties. His plastic or fibre shell chairs were in tune with the times, getting their inspiration from nature (animals, bubbles) or the everyday world of objects (tablets, toys). His Globe chair (1964, opposite, top right) fitted into the world of James Bond and Dr No perfectly. While the Pony chair (1973, opposite, bottom right) illustrated just how far from Constructivist ideals a piece of furniture could go.

Finnish designer **YRJÖ KUKKAPURO** (born 1933) was also influenced by the free spirit of the 1960s, as shown in his Karuselli easy chair (1965, bottom left) in fibreglass and leather. Unlike Aarnio though, Kukkapuro has always aimed to combine Constructivist and organic ideals in his furniture design. The Karuselli easy chair is still in production by Inno Avarte.

Danish designer **VERNER PANTON** (1926–98) was the great pioneer of organic design. Originally working in tandem with Arne Jacobsen, Panton is said to have had decisive influence on the final shape of the Ant chair (see p. 90). His own success came later, after he moved abroad in the 1960s. The Cone chair (1958, right) belongs to his early work. The Panton chair (1967) is still the prime icon of plastic furniture and is produced today by Vitra.

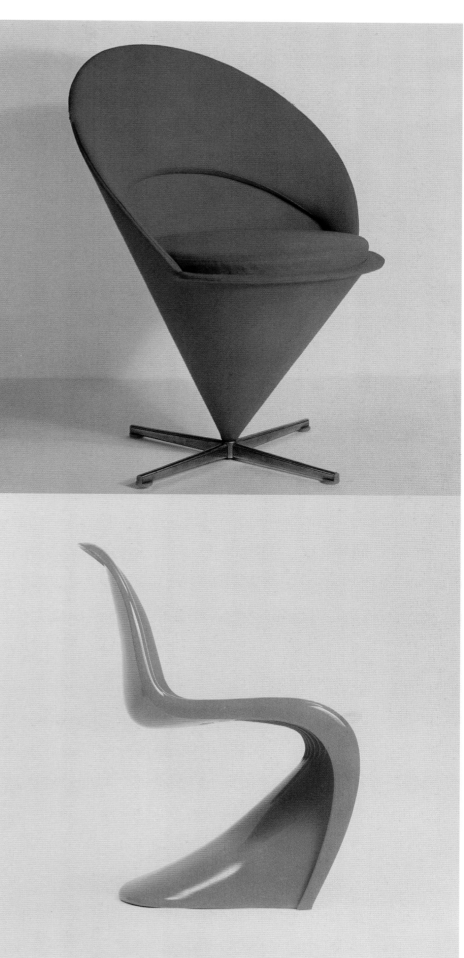

Norwegian designer **OLAV ELDØY** has given the Stokke world of ergonomic ideals a playful twist in the fruit-inspired Peel easy chair.

Stokke chairs, ergonomically designed in cooperation with medical expertise to enhance an unconventional but more ideal body carriage while at work, are an important Norwegian gift to modern design. The Stokke original by Norwegian designer **PETER OPSVIK** has one seat for the behind, two for the knees.

Danish designers **BORIS BERLIN** and **POUL CHRISTIANSEN** of Komplot Design, used rubber for their Non chair (above), which makes it suitable for use outdoors. It is manufactured by Källemo.

Finnish designer **SARI ANTTONEN** often uses recycled materials in his designs and has taken part in the construction of the Eco-Logis environmental building. With his prize-winning chair Kiss, however, only the name touches nature.

Swedish designer **MONICA FÖRSTER** works innovatively with materials and functions, constructing rooms with inflatable textiles and letting light pass through rubber, so that it resembles an object from outer space. The material she used for her Silikon lamp, which is manufactured by David Design was moulded silicone

Big Hug is the name given to the armchairs in this series by Swedish designer **ANNA VON SCHEWEN** and manufactured by Gärsnäs. The frame in constructed from sold bent beech on powder coated steel tubing, with or without (as in this image) upholstered arms.

The influence of Verner Panton's uncompromising organic furniture can be traced in Swedish designer **ANJA SEBTON**'s daring Add one + two sofa for Lammhults. Based around a steel frame, the sofa's seats and backs are constructed from plywood with injected polyurethane foam shaping it's pregnant form.

The Panton connection is underlined when Sebton's Add one sofa is upholstered with the Danish design icon's 1960 textile Geometric.

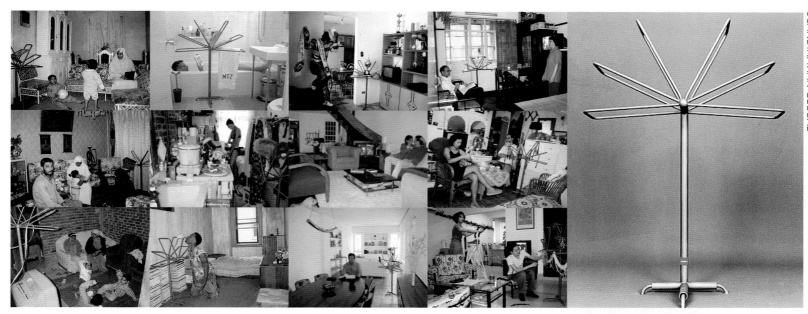

Global One. Swedish designer **SANNA HANSSON**'s bird-like magazine rack is not just an object, but a story about interacting cultures. After completing the rack the designer travelled around the world, documenting how families in different countries saw and chose to use the rack.

Global Two. For the younger generation there are few national barriers. The classic Scandinavian simplicity is blended with sleek, minimal, international influences, as in Swedish designer **MONICA FÖRSTER**'s Tray side table (below), which is manufactured by Offect.

More global. Many contemporary Scandinavians have their designs produced by high-profile international companies. Also Scandinavian producers work more closely with well-known international designers. Swedish architect **EERO KOIVISTO**, the designer behind the table series DNA, does both: he works for prestigious Italian companies such as Cappellini, and helps Swedish producers such as Swedese and Offecct to cooperate with international designers such as James Irvine, Karim Rashid and Jean-Marie Massaud.

The Finnish architect's studio **VALVOMO** had a great international breakthrough with their Snowcrash show at the international furniture fairs in Milan and Cologne in the late 1990s. Among Valvomo's later successful products are the Soundwave acoustic wall tiles.

The flow of Scandinavian designs crossing borders steadily grows. From the left: Frank chair designed by **ANDREAS ENGESVIK** from the design group **NORWAY SAYS**; Air, a series of blow-up furniture designed by **JAN DRANGER** for Ikea; Glowblow, a lamp designed by **VESA HINKOLA**, **MARKUS NEVALAINEN** and **RANE VASKIVUORI** of the Valvomo studio; Apollo sofa table designed by **ALEXANDER LERVIK** for Sputnik; and Dranger's Air again.

The most interesting part of Danish designers **BORIS BERLIN**'s and **POUL CHRISTIANSEN**'s Non rubber chair is its underside. Turned upside down this "non-design" piece of furniture contains a message to the world.

Finnish designer **ILKKA SUPPANEN**'s Flying carpet sofa (above) was part of the original Snowcrash and Valvomo presentation in Milan. Suppanen's beautifully simple structure gained immediate international attention; it is produced by Cappellini.

The famous Nordic light, with a futurist twist. Norwegian design team **HELEN AND HARD**'s prized coloured lights are in fact little wax lamps equipped with fibre optics.

INTERIORS

We have all seen them. The charming, bright interiors with light flooding through thin, white curtains – rooms in which each piece of furniture and every object appear essential and functional, where the fresh wild flowers in a beautiful vase on the table seem to have been picked from the grassy verge outside, and where the whole scene is imbued with comfort and beauty.

That is exactly what it looked like in the homes of well-known Nordic artists, which have been seen so often in pictures. Perhaps the best known is Carl and Karin Larsson's home at Sundborn in Dalecarlia, which was immortalized in the international best-seller, *A Home* (1899). Then there is the work of the Danish painter P S Krøyer who, in the late nineteenth century, painted scenes of the most famous fishing village of the "Nordic light", Skagen. Among his work is *Kunstnerfrokosten* (*The Artists' Lunch*), which portrays a languid group of artists sitting around a table that is mostly covered in bottles and glasses. The scene is a simple room in the legendary Brøndum hotel and conveys a sense of ease and satisfaction. Then there is Hvitträsk, the home of the Finnish architect Eliel Saarinen just outside Helsinki, which is a well-conceived manifestation of Scandinavian Arts and Crafts that still arouses admiration.

These artists' homes strike a clear Scandinavian chord that has had enormous importance, not least for Scandinavians themselves when it comes to furnishing their homes. For even if Functionalism spread over a wide front in Scandinavia at the end of the 1920s, it did not mean that everybody immediately followed the fashion. In fact, the opposite is true. Even if it was easy for the whole fraternity of young, radical

architects to adopt these ideas about mass production quickly – working with glass, steel and concrete – then ordinary people were more conservative, to put it mildly.

Scandinavians have, however, always been drawn to the hearth, a result of the cold outdoor climate and the sparse population. Norway and Iceland have the lowest population densities in Europe, an average of just 14 people per square kilometre. Neither have these northernmost countries had the same village structure as the rest of Europe, instead the population inhabited solitary farms with long distances in between. Isolation was the norm, and people concentrated on making their homes as comfortable possible. Norwegian sociologist Kjetil Rolness, who thoroughly researched his countrymen's furnishings during the twentieth century in his book *Med smak skal hjemmet bygges* (*With Taste Shall the Home be Built*, 1995), maintains that Norwegians go as far as not wanting to have their neighbours within view. Instead they prefer plenty of space in their homes, something that is confirmed by the fact that eighty per cent of them live in detached houses, a figure well above that for the other Nordic countries.

Compared with the rest of Europe, socializing takes place in the home rather than in a restaurant or bar. This gives Scandinavians an even greater impetus to create domestic environments that are as congenial as possible. It also explains why Scandinavian home furnishings can be viewed as a sort of popular art, something that Rolness underlined. The most important aim was to create an environment in which all feel comfortable and for which they care. Interiors became a form of personal expression, a trend that increased

steadily during the twentieth century. Rolness goes so far as to say that this "aesthetification of everyday life" is a decisive and slightly underestimated activity in today's consumer society: "Never before in history has artistic creativity been so widely rooted in people's everyday lives than it is today."

At the same time this form of popular art has often become a battlefield in which fierce struggles have taken place between good or bad taste. An intensive public debate broke out with the breakthrough of Functionalism. The state, professional architectural associations and, to a certain extent, the rising design media took it upon themselves to teach the populace how to appreciate International Style, improve their taste and furnish their homes correctly. All participated in these massive educational campaigns. Major exhibitions were organized where new ideas and visions for the home were displayed. Even science jumped on the bandwagon. Through wide-ranging housing surveys, researchers were able to find out how outmoded and "incorrectly" people arranged their homes, following up their findings with blunt instructions as to what they should look like.

The scientific view was particularly triumphant in the kitchen. The argument here was not about opinions and taste but about measurable units such as hygiene, safety and security. Innumerable standardized kitchen fittings, planned down to the smallest detail and millimetre, appeared in the middle of the nineteenth century and made their breakthrough in the major building programmes after the Second World War.

Architects became a sort of advice panel who – when it came to home furnishings – seemed to have been commissioned more by society than by individuals. On the other hand they worked professionally with

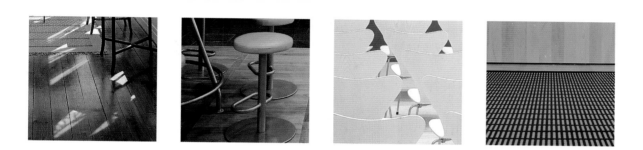

public interiors. For a long time it was primarily public spaces, such as cultural and political meeting areas, where architects' visions became reality, but to an increasing degree this occurred in commercial contexts such as restaurants, shops and offices.

Architecturally drawn interiors have enjoyed a boom since the late 1980s. In office environments, ideas of the most up-to-date and persuasive architectural expressions interplay with economically motivated philosophies around corporate identity. Many of the Nordic interiors that have attracted the most attention in recent years were conceived as corporate commissions, and were aimed at strengthening a company's visual identity through architecture. For example the Scandinavian airline SAS commissioned a new image for its lounges and tax-free shops around the world and the Finnish telecom giant Nokia invested many millions in its stylish new head office outside Helsinki.

Restaurants are another sector where interiors have become even more conceptual. In the Nordic countries there are, as in other urban centres around the globe, a succession of trendy and exquisitely appetizing restaurant environments, that are often short lived. But there are also notable classics. For example the Finns have managed to keep a remarkable number of genuine, functional environments, restaurants and bars alive that are excellent meeting places and are now characterized by a comfortable cordiality. For the Danes on the other hand the classic restaurant is a crowded beer hall, timelessly simple and aesthetic. Or brand new, such as Jacobsen, the restaurant built adjacent to the Bellevue Theatre outside Copenhagen. Designed by Arne Jacobsen in the 1930s, it is furnished throughout with his famous touch, a place that stands out as a modern setting of the architect's combined works. In Sweden, the newly furnished Sturehof illustrates another approach to this prized classic phenomenon.

Classic Scandinavian Modernism:
two legendary **ARNE JACOBSEN**
interiors. The Bellevue Theatre (left) is
still in existence, however, the lobby
of the SAS Royal Hotel in Copenhagen
(above) looks very different today.
The hotel was built between 1956 and
1961, and was the original setting for
the Egg and Swan chairs (see p. 90)
The considerably older interior of
the Bellevue Theatre (1932–35)
in Klampenborg, north of Copenhagen,
has been carefully restored. With their
undulating backs, the chairs of the
auditorium marked the beginning of
Jacobsen's use of steam-bent plywood.

Organic style from the 1970s. Danish
architect **VERNER PANTON** (1926–98)
was one of the most colourful and
innovative postwar designers. His
legendary interiors for restaurants
and clubs, such as the Varna restaurant
in Arhus, Denmark (below, 1971)
are milestones in the history of
European design. Panton created his
organic interiors as landscapes, the
walls, floors, furniture and textiles all
forming elements of a united whole.

Aalto and Jacobsen still
going strong. With its
striped balustrades of
white marble the
Academic Bookstore
in Helsinki was designed
in 1971 by Finnish
husband and wife **ALVAR**
and **ELISSA AALTO**. The
basic idea of the interior –
that one can see through
both each storey and
the building as a whole
– is still intact. The Arne
Jacobsen furniture
was a later addition.

Swedish Modern – light, refined and simple. Austrian architect **JOSEF FRANK**, who moved to Sweden in the 1930s, created a personal, much-loved version of Modernism. His textiles were often brightly coloured (unlike those in this interior), with large floral prints. His furniture, as can be seen here, was simple, elegant and easy to move. Frank believed that comfort, flexibility and close contact with nature were important qualities in the home.

Unmistakably Scandinavian – the headquarters of Swedish bakery Pågen (opposite, 1968) were designed by British-born architect **RALPH ERSKINE** (born 1914), who moved to Sweden in 1939. The interior is generously furnished with well-known Nordic classics. This relaxed conference room contains **YRJÖ KUUKKAPURO**'s Karuselli chair (1965, see p. 101) and Danish designer **POUL HENNINGSEN**'s Pigna lamp (1958), which was originally designed for a restaurant at Langelinie in Copenhagen.

Finnish designer **ANTTI NURMESNIEMI** (born 1927) designed the sauna of the Palace Hotel in Helsinki (above, 1951) as part of a project that Finnish architect Viljo Revell was commissioned to design. The sauna is a clearly modern interpretation of the Nordic rite of the sauna. The room's little wooden stool, which is both innovative and traditional, has become a classic (see p. 82).

The blonde wooden interior is as striking in today's contemporary homes as it is in Finn Juhl's 1940s house. In this interior, designed by Stockholm- and London-based architect **SHIDEH SHAYGAN**, the dining chairs and table were designed in 1947 by Danish architect **BØRGE MOGENSEN** and PH5 pendant lamp was created by Danish architect **POUL HENNINGSEN** in 1958. The effect is not nostalgic – in fact it is quite the opposite.

Architect and furniture designer **FINN JUHL** was one of the Danish masters, working in a sophisticated manner, and inspired by abstract art and sculpture. In the early 1940s he built his own house in Klampenborg north of Copenhagen (left), everything but the paintings and homeware within it were of his own design – the house, the furniture and the textiles. As is typical in Denmark, where wood is frequently used and the traditional skills of the cabinetmaker are respected, the floors are treated in a soft and natural manner, simply soaked in lye and soaped.

Finnish architect Alvar Aalto's friends Maire and Harry Gullichsen were the clients for his renowned Villa Mairea (1939, see also p. 22) in Noormarkku. The interiors of this influential piece of architecture together created a hand-crafted *Gesamtkunstwerk*.

Much later Maire Gullichsen's son, the architect **KRISTIAN GULLICHSEN** (born 1932) designed a family house in Provence, a simple building made for outdoor life. His mother was a central figure in the Finnish design world, and was the driving force behind institutions such as the Artek shop and gallery in Helsinki and the Finnish Modern Arts Association. Her impeccable taste and skill, meant that she was a vital ambassador for Finnish design culture.

The Busk house, which was designed by Norwegian architect **SVERRE FEHN,** is tuned to the changes of the seasons and the time of the day. Built on a wooded, stony ridge in southern Norway the owners could start their day with the morning light at the northeast end of the house and finish it at sunset around the fireplace at the building's west end. The architecture of Sverre Fehn, who won the international Pritzker prize in 1997, is inspired by the landscape, which is also highly evident from the interior.

A strong theme in Nordic architecture in recent years has been the airport. Many ambitious projects have been realized, among them Oslo's Gardermoen airport (opposite), which was designed by Norwegian architects **AVIAPLAN**. The ambition was to create a Nordic tranquillity with the interiors. Calm surfaces, natural materials, light, simplicity and clarity in layout are the major design features.

The lounges for the Scandinavian airline SAS (above and right) were given a distinctly Nordic feel by the designs **THOMAS ERIKSSON** implemented in the late 1990s. The interiors of the lounges are light and homely, informal and highly functional. They represent a modern update of the Scandinavian design ideal for airports all over the globe, such as here at Stansted, near London.

Previous pages: the work environment of tomorrow. Swedish architects **THAM VIDEGÅRD HANSSON** designed this unconventional office in Stockholm, which was fitted exclusively with technologically and functionally advanced furniture designed by the Finnish architecture studio **VALVOMO**.

Stylish and clean. Swedish architect **THOMAS ERIKSSON** designed the interiors of the London-based magazine *Wallpaper* with subdued colours and lots of wood. As is common in Eriksson's interiors, the furniture chosen for the offices is an international mix, with pieces across the board from Arne Jacobsen to Jasper Morrison, however, the impression given is still distinctly Nordic. The black and white carpet was designed by the architects.

Romantic. The Sturehof restaurant in Stockholm is more than a hundred years old. In the 1990s the building's interiors, including two dining rooms and five bars, were overhauled by Swedish architect and designer **JONAS BOHLIN**. He spent several years on the project, discovering engraved glass walls from almost a century ago in the storerooms and using them together with his own contemporary designs. The multi-coloured tulle lamps and heavy iron and leather chairs in the upper bar are examples of the latter.

Overleaf: **CLAESSON KOIVISTO RUNE** designed the offices for industrial design group No Picnic (see also p.134).

Icelandic Modern. Architects **STUDIO GRANDA** had great success during the 1990s, designing a string of landmark public buildings for Reykjavik. Among them Reykjavik City Hall (opposite) with its dramatically lit auditorium. Sliding wooden doors, strong geometric appearances and colours characterize the top floors of the Iceland Supreme Court (above). In the lobby of the Reykjavik Art Museum (below) volumes, surfaces and light create a raw and monumental impression.

Page 129: basic values, and a Minimalist approach to the carpentry tradition. A detail of the wooden interior of the Izakaya Koi restaurant in Malmö, which was designed by Swedish architect **JONAS LINDVALL**.

Close to nature, Nordic. The light and flexible ideals of **JOSEF FRANK** (see p. 115) from the early twentieth century still linger in the interior of this contemporary summer-house, designed by Swedish architect **ANNA VON SCHEWEN** (opposite). In the lower right corner of the image a glimpse of von Schewen's Latta chair can be seen.

Close to nature, global. Danish architect **KIM UTZON** has lived all over the world, and the influences from many cultures shows in his own house in Ålsgårde. In the construction of the house, which was designed and built by Utzon, ordinary telephone poles have been used as load bearing.

Basic values, volume and light were the aim when Swedish architects **CLAESSON KOIVISTO RUNE** designed the offices for industrial design group No Picnic (see also p.128).

The Vistet catalogue house, designed by Swedish architects **ANDERS LANDSTRÖM** and **THOMAS SANDELL**, is part of a project in which modern design is applied to traditional timber techniques. This Vistet house interior, an exhibition display, is also furnished with items by the various young Swedish designers.

Finnish forms, transparent. Helsinki's New Opera House, which was built between 1987 and 1993 by architects **HYVAMAKI, KARHUNEN & PARKKINEN**, evokes the coolness of the characteristic Scandinavian style.

Finnish forms, massive. Wood throughout – even the carpet comes from the woods,

and is woven from paper yarn (see also p.55).

No other craft conveys the contrast between nature and culture in Scandinavia more dramatically than the art of jewellery; in fact the craft could be perceived as having two diametrically opposed directions today. One is abstract, austere and influenced by Modernist expressions, while the other is more liberated, expressive and colourful, with its roots in the ancient popular culture of the region. Take, for example, the geometric, restrained, yet powerful work in silver and felt by Pia Wallén and Maria Elmqvist, or Per Suntum's austere brooch in reconstructed coral and gold, or Ari Turunen's brooches in materials such as silver, marble and diabase. Compare them with Norwegian Liv Blåvarp's decorated neckpieces in painted wood, satin and ebony, or with Jón Snorri Sigurdsson's serpentine, uneven silver ring in which Icelandic lava takes the place of a conventional gem. There is little doubt this is the meeting of two worlds, both deeply rooted in Scandinavian culture.

Silver plate was one of the attractions when Scandinavian design made its breakthrough in the 1950s. Attention was focused primarily on designs from Georg Jensen's foundry, which had a long tradition in the craft. From Jensen's workshop came abstract and organic shapes by designers such as Henning Koppel and Nanna and Jørgen Ditzel. Since then the international wave of "New Jewellery" has made a major impact in the Scandinavian countries with its revolt against the conventions of the craft. New materials are blended with the old, "high" culture with "low", cheap with expensive – "gold and gum" was the catchphrase in Denmark in the 1980s. Hi-tech and synthetic materials such as titanium, PVC, acrylic, steel and aluminium were freely mixed with highly traditional gems as well as with local stone and wood. However, the chasm between nature and culture in Scandinavian jewellery design has remained.

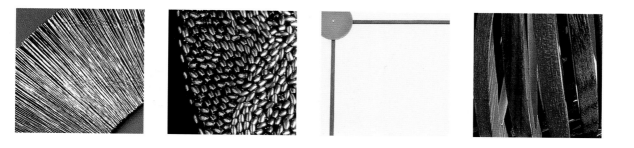

Originally, jewellery design was shaped by the different cultural backgrounds in the Scandinavian countries. The Danes came from a perspective that had more in common with the rest of Europe. An exclusive and internationally acclaimed jewellery culture was founded here at the turn of the twentieth century; however, in the other Nordic countries, jewellery design was shaped by an inherent asceticism and popular culture. The lack of ostentation in Scandinavian jewellery stemmed from both a lack of monarchical tradition and a strict Lutheran spirit that considered it reprehensible to adorn oneself.

Meanwhile, in late-nineteenth-century Denmark, architect Thorvald Bindesbøll and painter Harald Slott-Møller worked together with famous goldsmiths in Copenhagen. A decade later workshops were opened by Mogens Ballin, Evald Nielsen and the aforementioned Jensen. Together with artists and sculptors they created jewellery that was influenced by Art Nouveau and the Arts and Crafts movement with organic subjects such as animals and flowers decorating arabesques. Inspiration was sometimes drawn from contemporary international celebrities such as C.R. Ashbee and René Lalique; the latter was extremely influential for the Danes until the 1930s when Functionalism challenged this sort of decorative culture.

After the Second World War, Danish silver went on to further glory, not least in the collaboration of sculptor Henning Koppel and Jensen's silversmiths. Inspiration was drawn from contemporary abstract art, particularly sculptors such as Jean Arp and Henry Moore. The Danes also experimented with materials such as ceramic, glass, wood, amber and ivory. What Christian Dior was for the New Look in 1947, Koppel was for modern

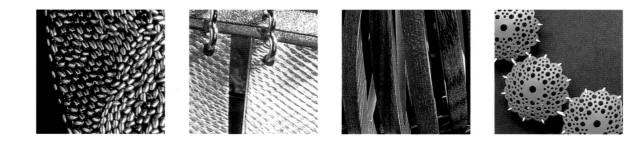

Danish silverwork. As art historian Lars Dybdahl commented, "Koppel – like Alvar Aalto – managed to balance a fascination with the organic expressiveness of curved natural lines with an urban, modernistic simplification."

In Sweden and Finland there were also strong links between jewellery design and contemporary abstract painting and sculpture. In 1958 a revolutionary exhibition was held at Aalto's furniture studio Artek in Helsinki, which elevated silver to the same level as other Finnish design. It was characterized by the use of stones from the Finnish countryside, and simple abstract shapes without any historical influence, distinct structures or logical construction.

Jewellery played a modest role in Swedish design, but a few of the leading silver and goldsmiths succeeded in making a strong impression when Scandinavian Style first came to international attention. Wiwen Nilsson was a pioneer who, during the 1930s, had been impressed by international Modernism in the form of *Neue Sachlichkeit* and cubist paintings. One of his early students was Sigurd Persson who made his breakthrough at the end of the Second World War with dramatic but cleanly designed necklaces and rings. In turn he inspired Torun Bülow-Hübe who made her debut in 1948 and then became one of the greatest Scandinavian jewellery designers of the post-war period, working for Georg Jensen since 1967.

Conditions for the Norwegians and Icelanders were different. Tradition has been one of the strongest driving forces in both these countries, opening the way for powerful, distinctive and colourful expressions in jewellery design. The most important contribution from Iceland was the threaded and plaited filigree work, which reached its peak in terms of variety and skilful workmanship in the eighteenth century and continued to dominate well into the twentieth century.

There may have been no aristocracy in Norway to influence the development of jewellery, but there was a rich and peculiar tradition of adorning the folk costumes. The aim for the Norwegian silversmiths at the beginning of the twentieth century was to recapture the nation's heritage, and jewellery design played a decisive role here. The distinctive "dragon" style developed, influenced by medieval patterns; enamel was also utilized, using rich colours in keeping with Norwegian art. A leading Norwegian jewellery maker, who first came to prominence in the 1920s, was Sigurd Alf Eriksen. His work was described as baroque, and was in stark contrast to contemporary Scandinavian ideals, which were characterized by moderation and simplicity. His successors in Norwegian jewellery making created expressive, rough jewellery, sculptured quality and varied texture – all typical for the craft in the twentieth century. However, there were Norwegian representatives of the prevalent school of clean lines in the Scandinavian design of the 1950s, primarily Grete Prytz Kittelsen. She experimented, almost scientifically, in her search after new knowledge, new enamels and her own, hitherto unproven, techniques. Through the years she was involved in many innovative projects, working with silver and glass. Among the companies she worked for were the Italian company Venini.

"New Jewellery" also made an especially strong and early breakthrough in Norway where the freer and more complex stance coincided with ideas that had characterized all Norwegian household articles in the 1970s. There was also considerable ethnic inspiration from objects such as feathers, glass beads, colourful threads and beans. Today this approach to jewellery design is used throughout the Nordic countries with a vigorous and experimental direction without exception. "Portable art" is the aim rather than "portable prosperity", that is to say, status symbols. Imagination is unlimited when it comes to new materials. In Finland, which is rich in paper-producing forests, torn paper and corrugated cardboard are frequently used, while Icelanders employ pieces of volcanic rock from their landscape.

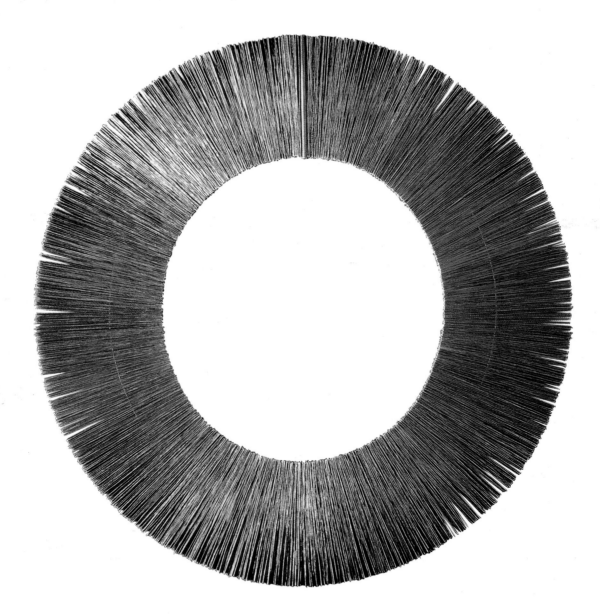

This page and opposite: silver necklaces by Norwegian designer **TONE VIGELAND**. The free spirit of the "New Jewellery" boomed in the Nordic countries during the 1990s, mixing traditional Scandinavian craft values with strong experimental attitudes. All the pieces shown within this chapter have been exhibited at the Nordic Jewellery Triennales, which have been held since 1995.

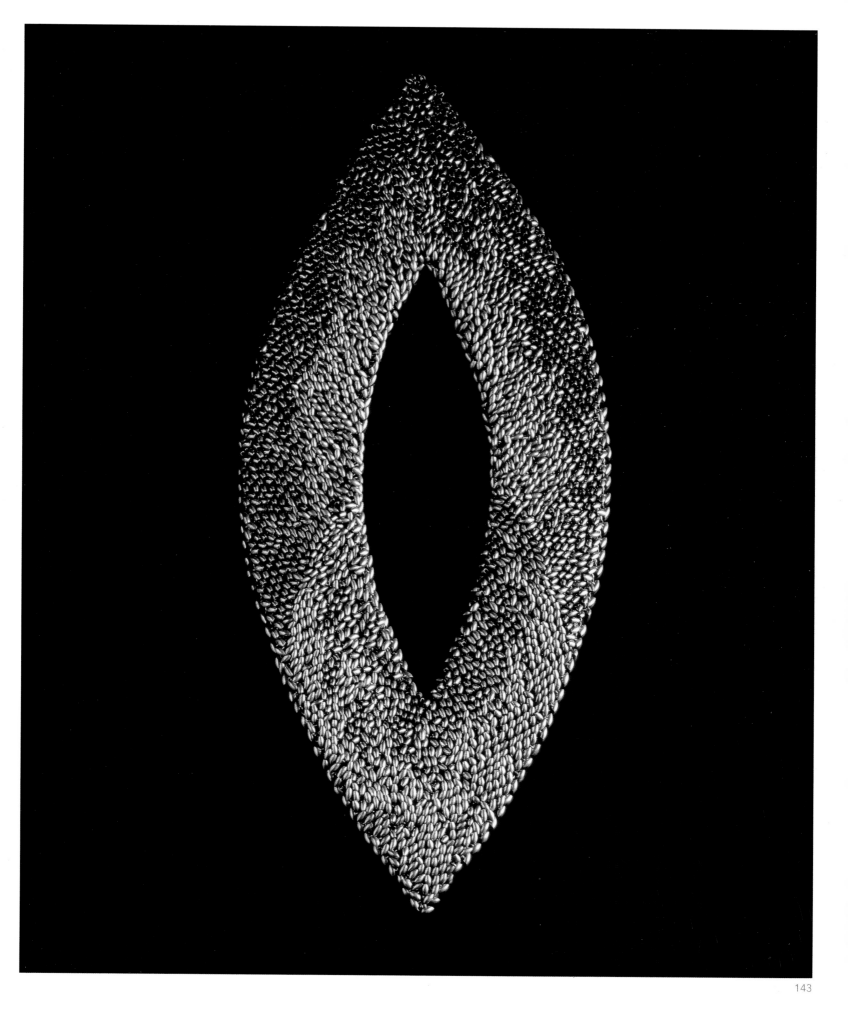

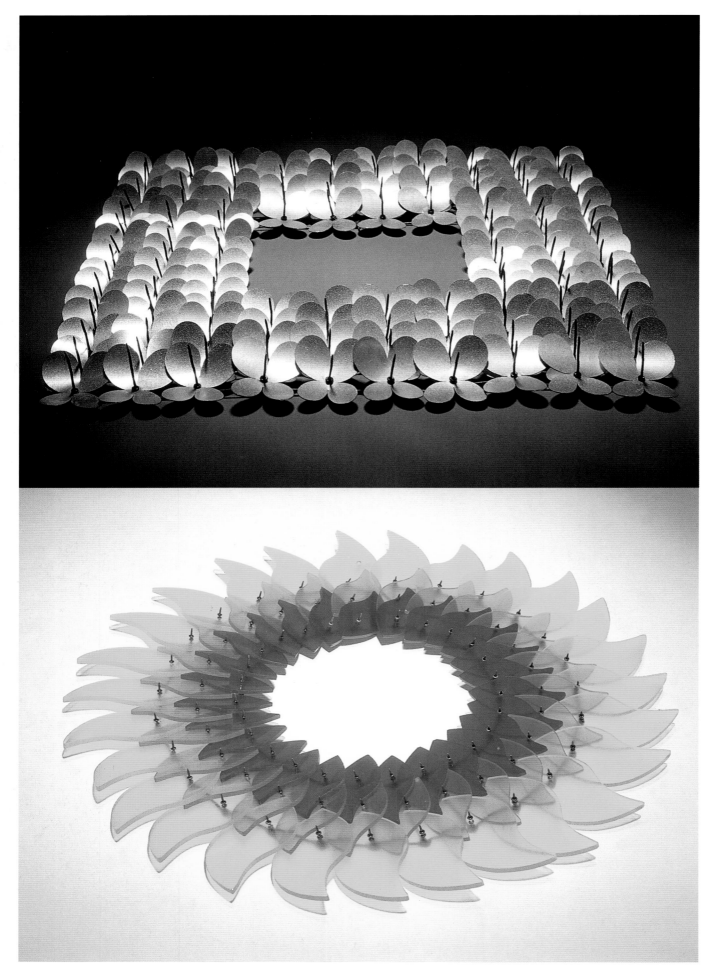

The Norwegian designer **JANICKE HORN** uses traditional jewellery metals such as copper, silver and gold, but subjects them to various untraditional surface treatments. For example the metal has been oxidized in the ring at the top of the page.

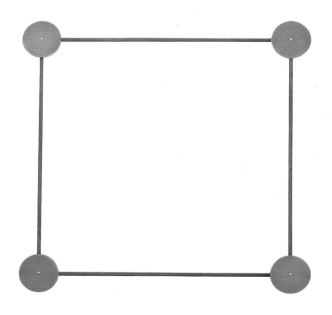

Necklace in iron, niobium and gold by Swedish silversmith **TORE SVENSSON**. He started experimenting with iron in the early 1980s, working with the metal as though it was the more malleable silver.

Above and below: brooches in silver and gold by Danish designer **PEDER MUSSE**. His pieces of jewellery resemble sculptures, telling a story or relating to a sensual, humorous or emotive experience.

Bracelet in gold, silver and nylon by Danish designer **KASIA GASPARSKI**. She finds inspiration for her delicate works in submarine creatures, organic growth and in the cell structures of microscopy.

Finnish designer **HELENA LEHTINEN** uses bone, wood and other natural materials in her jewellery designs, which are combined with delicate engravings in gold.

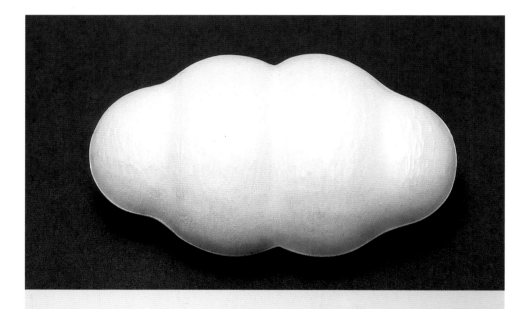

Brooches by the Norwegian designer **SYNNØVE KORSSJØEN** who works with enamel in an unusual way. After firing, the enamel is filed, which gives the surface a rougher look.

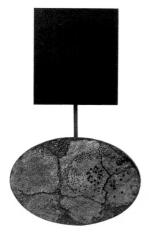

Finnish designer **ARI TURUNEN** constructs pieces of jewellery as if they were miniature sculptures, using natural materials such as diabase, marble, quartz and ebony, often in combination with silver.

Danish designer **ANNETTE KRAEN** mixes inspiration from Nordic nature with influences from the East. This delicate brooch is fashioned from oxidized silver, lacquer and gold leaf.

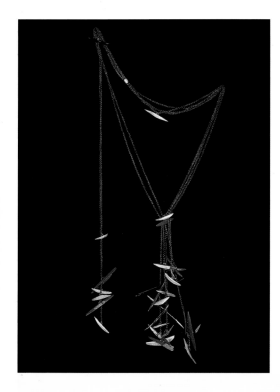

The Danish designer **PER SUNTUM** experiments with the chemistry of his materials and their interaction with other elements, giving his delicate pieces, such as these brooches (above and below) an intriguing identity of its own.

Neckpiece by Norwegian artist **LIV BLÅVARP**, who uses unusual materials such as birch, palisander, lemon wood and ebony.

Although her pieces are strong and independent objects in themselves, they are definitely intended to be worn.

Neck collar in tombac, a copper alloy, by
Norwegian designer **HILDE E DRAMSTAD**.

Necklace in gold by the Swedish metalsmith
CECILIA JOHANSSON.

"For the Black": a necklace in acrylic and silver
by Norwegian designer **INGER MARIE BERG**.

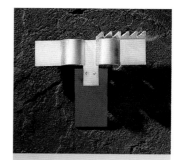

An innovative brooch in silver, gold and titanium by the Danish designer **JAN LOHMANN**.

Finger sculpture in copper, gold and steel by the Danish designer **KIRSTEN CLAUSAGER**.

Danish designer **EVA DORA LAMM**'s jewellery is also supposed to be viewed as constructed spatial art.

Armring fashioned from silver and felt by Swedish textile designer **PIA WALLÉN** in collaboration with Swedish silversmith **MARIA ELMQVIST**.

Necklace in silver by Danish designer **THORKILD THØRGERSEN**. Her work finds its inspiration in ancient cultures all over the world, as well as in the purest of geometric forms.

For one week every spring the streets of Copenhagen are transformed from a quaint and historic tourist attraction into the scene of a full-blown fashion show. The Danish capital's Fashion and Design Festival has been run since the beginning of the 1990s. In contrast to the majority of other fashion shows throughout the world, it is a lively, popular event aimed at a wide audience, rather than merely aimed at the fashion elite. Within the setting of a medieval church young designers and established names, both Danish and international, show off their creations. Stylish shows are interlaced with debates, exhibitions and prize-giving ceremonies. At times the city centre's famous pedestrian street, Strøget, seems more like a catwalk.

Fashion has never played a leading role in Scandinavian design. However, since the 1990s a rebellious glamour has appeared in the northern latitudes. The Danish have been at the forefront of this movement, creating clothes that are both individual and sophisticated, elements that are illustrated by the festival. In the media they talk about the "Copenhagen Radicals", a group of promising, creative fashion designers with their own labels, who have received acclaim at home and abroad. Among these young fashion designers are Gurrh Burrh, Peter Jensen, Daughters of Style and Baum und Pferdgarten. The talents of two designers in particular, Praxis and >double w<, have been celebrated as fashion shows in Paris and London, and both are frequently seen in the international fashion press from *Vogue* to *Dazed & Confused*.

Until recently few northern stars have succeeded in the extremely tough world of international fashion, although there are two notable exceptions, the Norwegian Per Spook, who worked with both Christian

Dior and Yves Saint Laurent before starting his own fashion house in Paris in 1977, and Dane Erik Mortensen, the creative leader at Balmain since 1982. However, since the beginning of the 1990s their shoes have been filled by new talents like Anja Vang Kragh at Galliano and Roy Krejberg at Kenzo. There are also a handful of Scandinavians who have become internationally established with their own labels, they include Danes Uffe Frank (who works in Milan), Bruuns Bazaar, Munthe and Simonsen, and J Lindeberg; and Swedish designers Marcel Marongiu in Paris and Richard Bengtsson in New York (who created the name Richard Edwards together with Edward Pavlick).

A completely different kind of fashion than that associated with French couture was created by two women – Katja of Sweden and Vuokko Nurmesniemi, the designer behind the Finnish Marimekko collection. The work of these two designers was typical of Scandinavian fashion ideas, with strong links to Nordic furniture design and architecture. Both women achieved fame during the 1960s with simple lines and comfortable garments that often used striking patterned fabric. Their fashions were adored by women and were sometimes labelled – in true democratic tradition – feminist. Just as with Coco Chanel, Katja of Sweden developed her own revolutionary fabric, in this case 3T-jersey (Tvätta-Torka-Tapå, which roughly means wash 'n' wear). The candid Scandinavian approach was typified by Nurmesniemi's statement that "a woman is sexy, not the dress".

A hint of the austere Nordic soul is discernable in the new wave of Swedish fashion designers that became well known in the 1990s. The creations of Anna Holtblad, Pia Wallén and Nygårds Anna all have their roots

in typical Scandinavian design, from the timelessly elegant to a modern version of pure folklore. And another generation of daring Swedes has since appeared on the fashion scene with individual representatives such as Louisa Burfitt and Roland Hjort, the latter with the Whyred label. Young avant-garde designers are also to be found in Finland with labels such as Ivanahelsinki, designed by Paola Ivana Suhonen and Lustwear, designed by Maikku Mettinen, although they have not succeeded in the international sphere to the same extent as their Swedish counterparts.

Norwegian and Icelandic fashions have a more romantic and folkloric ring, and they are often influenced by traditional knitting techniques and patterns. This can be seen in Solveig Hisdal's machine-knitted cardigans for Oleana, a sort of updated, prettier version of the Norwegian national garment *lusekoftan*. Another designer who works with knitted materials is Marit Eken Kalager, whose work is more modern, graceful and less restrained. The Icelandic version of the *lusekoftan* is called *lopapeysa* and is also a heavy, patterned knitted jumper or cardigan known abroad simply as the Icelandic jumper. The cultural clashes between old traditions and new, fast, modern living that are visible in contemporary Icelandic society are reflected in fashion where a collection like Vala Torfadottir's and Bjorg Ingadottir's Victorian influenced "wise man's clothing" appear extreme and unusual. A skirt that mimics romantic crinoline silhouettes is combined with a coarsely knitted, broadly striped shawl. Meanwhile, Steinunn Sigurd's thin, elegant, slightly pleated black garments in knitted black cashmere have taken many refined steps away from the substantial folksy techniques.

On the whole, Scandinavian fashion has been primarily distinguished by sportswear. Some of the best well-known Nordic names, such as Norwegian Helly Hansen, Finnish Reima and Rukka and Swedish Fjällraven,

focus on essential utilitarian garments like windproof jackets, skiing and hiking equipment for use in extreme countryside and weather. Helly Hansen in particular has concentrated on producing effective high performance garments, while at Reima and Rukka advanced research has taken place into the development of "intelligent" materials. Motorcycle clothing in Rukka's "Armatech" series, for example, is created to be completely watertight but still breathable. While Reima's Cyberia "Smart Garment" is based on both hi-tech research and the Inuit's ancient knowledge of how to protect themselves against extreme weather and cold. Fjällraven made its international breakthrough with its classic "Greenland" anorak in 1965, which was originally seen as somewhat nerdy garment and square, but became elevated to the status of international fashion icon in the progressive 1970s.

Scandinavian fashion is also notable for its everyday garments, which are good value and stylish. A number of popular brands are well known internationally, including Swedish Filippa K, Tiger and Björn Borg (which no longer has links with the former tennis champion but is still known for excellent swimwear and underwear. Other well-known brands include the Danish Sand, In Wear and Matinique, Carli Gray's Cottonfield and Jackpot, and the Finnish Avenue and Ril's.

Last but not least we should not forget H&M, Sweden's answer to Ikea in the realm of clothing, which expanded during the 1990s to include shops in fashion capitals such as Paris. (H&M has had a shop in the most popular London shopping area, Oxford Street, since the 1970s, and has now opened in a branch in New York.) During the course of the 1990s H&M has put increasing effort into their design, which has led to the chain's low-cost fashion improving in quality and becoming more thorough. More its own brand, less an imitation.

Un-Scandinavian classics. Fashion, particularly high fashion, was never an important arena for Scandinavian designers. Norwegian designer **PER SPOOK** is unique. Having worked with both Christian Dior and Yves St Laurent, he has built his own *haute-couture* house in Paris. These floating designs are from his 1991–92 collections.

The Scandinavian classic. The characteristic textile patterns and geometric lines of the Finnish fashion house **MARIMEKKO** are typical of Scandinavian Style from the grand old days. Founded in 1951, Marimekko was transformed into a trendy clothes line by creative director **VUOKKO NURMESNIEMI**. The company philosophy was anti-fashion, with unisex models, functional cuts and strong, graphic patterns, that resembled the Op- and Pop-cultures of the era. Since the late 1990s, Marimekko has had a resurgence in popularity, using legendary patterns, such as **MAIJA ISOLA**'s 1963 Melon fabric (above) to design simple, contemporary clothes.

159

Swedish Neomodernism, the fashion version. Since the early 1990s fashion design has become more prominent in Sweden. Designer **ANNA HOLTBLAD** combines Nordic tradition with contemporary fashion in a stylish way, and is one of the most successful of this generation of fashion designers.

Swedish designer **PIA WALLÉN**, like Marimekko, represents an anti-fashion approach that still catches the trends of the moment. Her primary material is felt, which she uses both for clothes and furniture. Coarse seams are deliberately visible, both on strictly shaped garments such as the anorak (top left) and felt slippers (above). She also fashions "jewellery" from the material (top right).

Scandinavian jeanswear: the everyday
version. Clothes from Swedish brand
FILIPPA K are urban, feminine and laid back.

Scandinavian jeanswear: the well-mannered version. Meticulously tailored
denim clothes as well as business suits characterize Swedish brand **TIGER**.

Scandinavian jeanswear: the exuberant version. Going out and getting noticed is the main aim when wearing outfits from the Swedish brand **J LINDEBERG**.

Copenhagen radicals: different. Danish fashion has flowered since the mid-1990s, and is not afraid of either the extremely normal or the utterly exotic. Danish designer **MADS NØRGAARD** mixes laid-back classics with chic details.

Copenhagen radicals: sophisticated. New Danish fashion displays a bursting bouquet of expressions and styles, that are both rebellious and glamorous. Danish designers **MUNTHE AND SIMONSEN** have made a name for themselves using rich patterns and delicate materials, sometimes with oriental influences.

Looking back to the 1970s. Swedish brand **WHYRED** is known for its creation of urban everyday wear with clashing, not too overstated inspirations. He: a soft guy in a mix and match sporty mood; she: a city girl, natural and comfortable.

Smart swimwear and underwear, both practical and flirty, describe the ambitions of the **BJÖRN BORG** brand, named after the Swedish tennis legend who started the company.

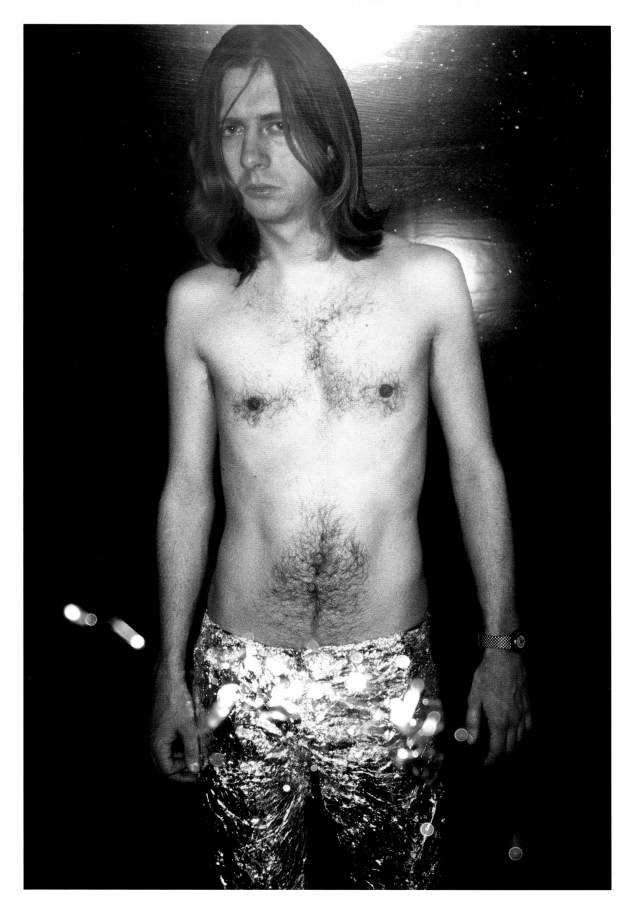

From the movies. **ACNE JEANS**, which are designed by Swedish creative collective Acne, fuse denim-based clothing with fashion. The Acne team works within film production, design and advertising. The group gets its inspiration from cinema, music and art.

Copenhagen radicals: glamourous. Danish designers **DAUGHTERS OF STYLE** strive for sumptuous effects, which are evident in their use of interesting details, such as embroidery, strategically shaped holes and pearls.

Copenhagen radicals: rebellious. Everyday elegance that is never boring characterizes the style of
Danish brand **BRUUNS BAZAAR**, which combines classic clichés with inventive details.

The rough climate of the north has made especially the Finns clever designers of outdoor clothing that is constructed to suffer the toughest of conditions. Outfits by the Finnish manufacturer **REIMA SMART CLOTHING** are designed for Arctic life and raw winter sports such as driving snowmobiles.

Protection, not only against the cold, but also from speed and the bitter wind, is given by the "intelligent" bodysuit from Finnish manufacturer **RUKKA**. The ultra-effective materials used in this kind of tough clothing is the result of hard scientific work and collaboration with university laboratories.

The Winter Olympics and other big sports competitions offer high profile opportunities to test the abilities not only of the participants but also of their equipment. Among them are outfits made for demanding conditions by manufacturers such as the Swedish **FJÄLLRÄVEN**.

Good design comes in many shapes and forms. The Cherrox children's rubber gumboot, sometimes looking even more colourful and animal-like than these six examples, make it fun to wear suitable footwear on a rainy day. Created by Norwegian designer **SIGRID ECKOFF** the cheery design of the Cherrox boot, made by Norwegian manufacturer Viking Fottöy, will seduce even the most reluctant child.

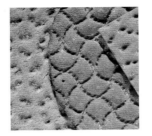

FOOD AND DRINK

As in other areas of Scandinavian life, the kitchen is also a place where old Nordic traditions and contemporary international aspirations come together. However, in the case of food and drink this is – in contrast to design and architecture – a relatively new phenomenon. It has little to do with artistic influences, instead being the result of the more urban lifestyle that took root in the Nordic countries during the last century. "Fusion" is the phrase used in today's fashionable cookery, which in Scandinavia means that traditional Danish, Swedish, Norwegian, Finnish and Icelandic methods are put into the blender with ideas from Mediterranean and Asian cuisines. To understand this eclectic approach requires a certain understanding of Scandinavian culinary roots.

Once again it is important to stress that these five countries do not form an obvious entity. There are thousands of kilometres from the south of Denmark to the North Cape, and with them a diverse range of climactic and cultural differences. Different historical influences from the bordering nations to the east, west and south of the Nordic nations have also affected eating habits. The culinary art of the Danes is richer and more varied than that of the other Scandinavians, and is characterized by bulging sausages, pork, goose and eel. On the other hand, the Finns have adopted delicacies such as *piroshki* and fermented bread from their mighty eastern neighbour, while the hardy inhabitants of the northern wilderness are the main consumers of such exotic delicacies as reindeer.

The long winters and short growing seasons are one thing all Scandinavians have in common, along with

the fact that their roots were as fishermen and hunter-gatherers. Their heathen forefathers were hardy fellows who had nothing against devouring fish, shellfish and game, raw or simply air-dried or smoked. In the eleventh century the Catholic Church tried to teach these wild northerners more civilized eating habits, and ordered change. The church decreed that no food should be consumed raw. However, this misfired as Scandinavians continued merrily with their highly edible and tasty "raw" methods of preservation. Something we should be grateful for today as *gravadlax* (raw salmon preserved with salt, sugar and dill) and raw herrings in a variety of sauces, are among the most appreciated delicacies from Scandinavia.

There are a profusion of berries in the forests of Norway that have always been picked and eaten; the simple red whortleberry and the bilberry have become a part of folklore and appear just as often in folksong as on the table. The Finns adore whortleberries stewed and thickened with potato flour, while in Sweden whortleberry preserve is part of the national heritage. In the northern bogs the expensive cloudberry is found, a fruit that is compared to gold, while in areas that can be cultivated, the sour Arctic raspberry is grown. Further south there are an abundance of rosehips, blackberries and sloes in the open pastureland where, according to ancient rights of way, anyone is allowed to pick them. The situation with vegetables on the other hand is not so good. Root vegetables, cabbage and turnip have been cultivated for centuries as they are able to survive in the fields for long periods. Peas and beans were also early arrivals as they were perfect for drying and became daily fare in such well-known specialities as pea soup and *bruna bönor*, which is a dish in which beans are cooked with syrup and vinegar.

The countryside, however, is more than woodland and fields where Scandinavians can pick and catch their daily bread, it is also their favourite place to lay their table. It goes without saying that you eat outdoors on a beautiful summer's day, and midsummer in June – when night and day are of equal length – is the ritual beginning for these lunches and dinners *al fresco*. It is then that typical light summer food forms a spread on the simple wooden table: herring accompanied by boiled potatoes that have been dug straight from the garden and smothered in chopped dill; freshly caught, cold poached salmon accompanied by a salad and a dessert of strawberries or rhubarb topped with whipped cream. All of which is washed down with a choice selection of spirit-based refreshments that seem to have an eternally mystical association with the pastoral northern countryside. A view of water is essential in this context, and there is an abundance of coastline and glittering lakes in Scandinavia to provide this. Fish from the ocean, rivers and lakes, has always been an important part of the Scandinavian diet – with cod, flatfish, mackerel, pike, perch and, of course, the fat and handsome salmon that swims up the rivers to breed, all popular.

However, the most important of all the fish to be found along the northern coasts is the herring. *Sill* is the name given to those caught off the western shores. On the Swedish east coast and in Finland these small, fat, slippery and glistening silver fish are known instead as *strömming*. There can be no other ingredient in the Scandinavian culinary canon that has given rise to such a wealth of distinctive preserved and cooked dishes each with its own fascinating name. A seemingly endless Finnish *strömming* table can include "cobbler's salmon" (preserved *strömming*), *strömming* rollmops, grilled *strömming*, *strömming* patties, *strömming* pasties, *böckling* (smoked *strömming*), *strömming au gratin* and *strömming* on potatoes. A Danish *sill* table on the other hand offers salted herring in sour cream, smoked herring, raw

salted herring rolled around a slice of gherkin and then pickled in spiced spirit vinegar, marinated salted herring and hardboiled egg, and fried salted herring. Swedish chef Tore Wretman gives thirteen recipes for *strömming* in a sauce or marinade in his book *Svensk Husmanskost* (*Swedish Home Fare*) as the start of the Swedish *smörgåsbord*.

The *smörgåsbord*, oh yes! This also has a long history. When the Scandinavian hunters and fishermen eventually began to cultivate the land and bake bread they found that stale bread could be made edible again by cooking it in ale, or it could be crumbled, buttered and covered with cheese or meat. This soon became the daily diet and the Scandinavian open sandwich, *smørrebrød* in Danish or *smörgåsen* in Swedish, was born. Eventually this led to the fabulous and sumptuous *smörgåsbord* banquet with its multitude of dishes, both hot and cold. In Finland they call it *Kalasbord*, (party table), while for the Norwegians it is *Koldtbordet* (cold table) – no hot dishes on the menu in other words.

At any of these tables, bottles dripping with condensation, and brimming full of spiced aquavit and beer are lined up in rows. The relationship between Scandinavians and alcohol is, however, complicated. It is a charged question characterized by hypocrisy and prohibition. Denmark is the only country where wines and spirits are freely available in shops, the rest have a state-run retail monopoly. At the same time several of them are skilful at manufacturing and marketing the forbidden fruit as is seen with Swedish *Absolut*, Norwegian *Löjtnens Linjeakvavit* and Icelandic *Svartír Dödenír* (Black Death). The more relaxed, perhaps less hypocritical Danes have cleverly marketed their beer culture abroad with well-known lagers such as Carlsberg and Tuborg.

Berries are vital in the cuisine of the Scandinavian countries, and fresh strawberries are an absolute must during the summer. They are eaten just as they are, with a little sugar and milk, with some whipped cream, with few drops of lemon, or used as filling in all kinds of cakes. A lot of time is spent in summer making juicy jams and syrups from seasonal fruits. Berries are not just beautiful and tasty, they are also healthy. For a child, around six strawberries provide more than one hundred per cent of the recommended daily intake of Vitamin C.

What could be more delicious? A typical Scandinavian summer cake with layers of meringue, whipped cream and handfuls of summer fruits.

Cloudberries – "gold of the north" – are rareties from the most northern regions of Scandinavia, where they grow on the boggy grounds of large pine woods. Redcurrants are more domesticated fruits, cultivated in gardens. Both types of berry are popular in traditional preserves and syrups.

Autumn is mushroom season. The Swedish love to walk out in the woods, equipped with big boots and baskets, picking all sorts of free-growing fungi. It is popular habit and requires good knowledge, as not all kinds of mushroom are edible – some of them are deadly poisonous. However, the golden chanterelle (above) is very safe. Easy to recognize, it is also easy to just clean, chop and eat. More delicious still are chanterelles fried in butter on a salad of oak leaf lettuce.

Berries are popular flavourings for simple syrups and cordials, which are mixed with water and served chilled on a hot summer's day. Hardly any other Nordic plant has been used for as many varied purposes as the elder. Partly toxic, it has been seen as both pathogenic and as a remedy and cure. Other culinary uses for the plant include tea from dried elderflowers and aquavit (see p.183) from the berries.

Many plants, such as asparagus (left) and greens (right) can be found growing wild, but are also grown industrially and in private gardens.

In Finland hearty soups of beetroot and potato – *borscht* – are a staple.

Nettles grow freely in large parts of Scandinavia, and were once an important raw material in poor households for use in soup, bread, tea and salads. Today nettles are seen as a more sophisticated ingredient; they are still used in soups, but also in soufflés or served with cheese and spaghetti, enhancing the flavour and adding colour. Nettles also have a long history as a folk remedy.

Rosehips can be made into a delicious preserve, and served on traditional Scandinavian dark bread.

Both sour and sweet tastes are typical in Scandinavian methods of preserving. Berries and fruits used for syrups and jams are of course mixed with large quantities of sugar for sweetness and preservation. But for vegetables such as cucumbers a combination of vinegar and sugar often is used, giving the pickled result a sharp, yet still distinctly sweet taste. A much saltier version of pickled cucumber is also available.

Fish, from the North Sea, from the Baltic and from the thousands of lakes in the Scandinavian countries, has always played an important role in the cuisine of the region. Cod, salmon and herring are among the most popular kinds of fish eaten, and they are prepared in numerous ways, although often they are cooked simply: boiled, fried or grilled. Smoked and pickled raw fish, especially salmon, are also Scandinavian specialities. Clockwise from the right: pickled salmon; a typical summer dish, herring with boiled potatoes; and "Toast Skagen" – prawns, mayonnaise and dill on a small slice of toasted white bread.

Onions, chives and leeks, are used to flavour herring fillets (above left). Herrings are also popular pickled with onions and dill (above). Prawns, crayfish and lobster are fished from Kattegatt and Skagerack on the North Sea (left, second left and far left). While eels are also a popular delicacy in Denmark (third left).

The traditional ways of smoking fish are still attractive (opposite).

Meatballs (far left) are one of the best-known Scandinavian cooking specialties, a necessity on the *smörgåsbord*. Sweden, Norway, Denmark and Finland have their own versions, these are made from elk meat. Reindeer is a popular meat, particularly in the northern regions of the Nordic nations (left).

Grouse shooting is an exclusive sport in the Northern mountains, resulting in exclusive dishes made from this game bird.

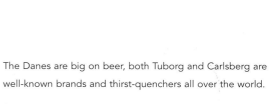

The Danes are big on beer, both Tuborg and Carlsberg are well-known brands and thirst-quenchers all over the world.

Scnapps and *sill* (herring) are absolute musts in all versions of the Scandinavian *smörgåsbord*.

Berries and spices are frequently used to flavour the numerous types of Scandinavian aquavits, which are the aromatic spirits of the region. Real aquavit lovers keep dozens of bottles in the larder seasoned with plants such as wormwood, elderberries or blackcurrants. Real aquavit lovers – and there are many in the north – keep dozens of bottles in the larder seasoned with plants or with berries.

Sweet bread for a coffee party. Cinnamon spirals sprinkled with lots of sugar are popular all year around, while buns flavoured with saffron and stuffed with raisins are more of a Christmas treat (left).

The Danes specialize in tasty rye bread, which, smothered with delicacies such as liver paté, bacon, smoked salmon, pickled herring and various cheeses, is perfect for the *smørrebrød*.

Crisp rye bread – *knäckebröd* – is a Swedish speciality, coming in many shapes and flavours. In northern parts of Scandinavia a thinner version of the crisp bread – *tunnbröd* – is popular.

Until the middle of the twentieth century, most of the baking for household needs was still done at home. Nowadays home-baking is reduced to the occasional cake – and even then it's often made with semi-manufactured ingredients.

Eating outside in the garden is a must during the short, bright summertime of the Nordic nations – at Midsummer the Sun hardly sets at all. The typical Midsummer menu contains pickled herring, sour cream, dill, freshly picked potatoes, aquavit and strawberries for dessert.

Christmas on the other hand is very much an indoor celebration, the long, dark hours lit by many candles. Traditional decorations made from straw and cut in pine wood dominate modern Christmas tables. Food of the season includes ham, pork ribs, pickled herring, boiled salt ling with sauce, and rice pudding (above). Saffron and raisin buns appear on the tables in early December (far left), as does mulled wine – *glögg* – with gingerbread (left).

Can a Scandinavian television claim to differ from a model made in Germany or Japan? It may seem an odd idea that the design of communication appliances, the most global of all products in today's media-oriented markets, should show national characteristics. But if, instead of a Scandinavian television, you talk about a Bang & Olufsen then the objections are not so obvious. The Danish manufacturer is in a league of its own in this area of product design and always has been. There is little to compare with a slimline Bang & Olufsen appliance, least of all in terms of its appearance; the question is whether the beautifully designed CD players and televisions are typically Scandinavian or just simply typical of their manufacturer.

The Scandinavian position is flexible and resilient; the Danish Wave exhibition that has toured the world since the end of the 1990s describes it as "a culture that has made the elaboration of the physical settings a matter of societal concern for almost a century, not as a specifically aesthetic, artistic discipline but as an integral part of the nation's economic and social development … as important as health, education, welfare and industrial policy." Even when it comes to the hi-tech present these established roots can be seen. Regional sensibility is quoted in the exhibition as one of the most important Danish characteristics, "treating the light as well as the local materials with respect for their textural qualities, combined with a concern for the environment."

The design teams at the Finnish firm Nokia or the Swedish companies Ericsson and Volvo may not choose to express themselves in quite this way when trying to put their finger on what is typically Scandinavian

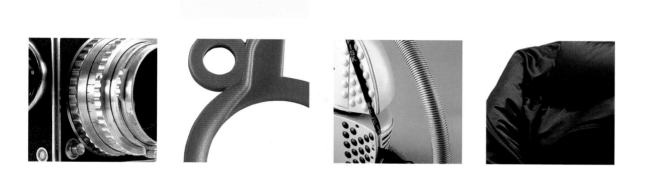

about their global products. However, whatever terms they used the meaning would be the same. When Ericsson launched its R320 phone they boasted proudly of "high quality materials and craftsmanship, function and comfort", which the company saw as the heart of the Scandinavian approach. And for the outsider there is no doubt. Nordic goods have a Nordic personality. In one of his first books *Cult Objects* (1985), Deyan Sudjic paid tribute to AGA stoves and Volvo cars, which he considered functional and reliable. Maybe not so smart and elegant but, as with the Volvo, "sturdy and sensible [and] styled to look safe too, with its intimidating bumpers and impossible to turn off headlamps. Not so much a motor car, more a way of life."

If you take a closer look you will see that these splendid Volvo cars and Ericsson telephones have been generated from the same sort of ethos as the other categories of product design. As with homeware and furniture, the emergent technological companies worked with artists during the first decades of the twentieth century to give their cars and telephones an interesting and self-assured design. In Volvo's case it was Helmer Mas Olle who came up with the basic ideas for the first models of the cars where the aim from the beginning was for a "conservative style" and "lasting beauty in the lines and proportions". Ericsson engaged Norwegian sculptor Jean Heiberg, who in 1931 created the first telephone in bakelite, which was then a modern material. This achieved cult status, becoming a legendary classic and the forerunner for all the devices in a variety of plastics that were made in the following decades, including the basic American model seen in so many black-and-white Hollywood films, which was created by design pioneer Henry Dreyfus at the end of the 1930s.

The job of industrial designer crept into the picture early, even if it was by the backdoor. Prince Sigvard Bernadotte of Sweden, an art graduate from Stockholm who became a silver designer at Georg Jensen in Copenhagen, spent many years in the United States during the 1940s, where he met several industrial design pioneers, including Dreyfus, Walter Dorwin Teague and Raymond Loewy. When several years later Bernadotte met the Danish architect Acton Bjørn, who also had an international background, having worked in the American aviation industry, they decided to confront Scandinavians with the concept of industrial design. Within a few years they had built up northern Europe's largest industrial design bureau with offices in Copenhagen and Stockholm and a considerable number of major Nordic companies as clients. All sorts of household machines and utensils were designed by the company – typewriters for Facit, calculators for Odhner, and a streamlined 1950s-style plastic dinner service for SAS. Many designers who later became famous began their careers with Bernadotte & Bjørn, including Jacob Jensen, who was the dominant profile at Bang & Olufsen during the 1960s and 1970s. Sigvard Bernadotte was also involved in campaign work at the highest level, for several years, was president of the International Council of Societies of Industrial Design (ICSID), which contributed to a more industrial view of the design that eventually took root in Scandinavia.

Today socially oriented subjects such as ergonomics, environmental awareness and aesthetically conscious production play a major role in Scandinavian industrial design. It is no coincidence that many of the technically advanced products that have received international acclaim over the past years for their design

are in fields such as medical appliances, equipment for the physically disabled, children's toys and environment-friendly power production. Neither is it by chance that considerable effort has been put into designing modern and convenient forms of transport and environments for public transport. New underground systems are, for example, being built or have recently been built in several of the Scandinavian capitals.

Even sport has stimulated a considerable amount of innovative Nordic design. Not least within cycling (a major sport in Denmark) and various winter sports for which Scandinavians already have the specialist knowledge. An apparently simple detail like the Avanti Aero Finnish skiing stick (1994), designed by Pasi Järvinen and Juha Kosonen, illustrates how this sort of product acquires an increasingly complex function. The significantly designed stick, the point of which resembles an elegant mini-wing, may be an aid for faster skiing. It certainly provides support but it also functions quite simply as a visual fashion signal in line with the skier's smart, protective sunglasses and tight clothes, designed to minimize air resistance. These sorts of master products have an increasingly stronger impact according to design historian Susann Vihma in the catalogue of the American exhibition *Modern Finnish Design* (1999). They are increasingly becoming trend-setters for products in completely different fields.

What could be more Swedish than the **VOLVO**? The 1960s P 1800 (below left) gained world fame in the television series *The Saint*, as the car of choice for suave detective Simon Templar (Roger Moore). Despite these glamorous connotations, maximum security and comfort have always been the key issues of the Volvo brand. In the 1990s the cars were stylish and sleek again, as can be seen in models such as the S80 (left), which was designed by **PETER HORBURY** and **JOSÉ DIAZ DE LA VEGA**.

SAAB cars had a revolutionary streamlined shape right from their inception in the 1940s. The first models were designed by **SIXTEN SASON** (1912–67) an ingenious, self-taught Swedish industrial designer. In the early twenty-first century Saabs such as the 9-3, are famous for their solid visual persona.

Bicycles are a big deal in Scandinavia, especially for the Danes. The **BIOMEGA** company, founded in the late 1990s by two philosophy students at the University of Copenhagen, develops and manufactures "urban" bicycles, such as the MN Extravaganza model (opposite), which was designed by Australian design star **MARC NEWSON**. Its key characteristic: an organically shaped frame that has been formed from aluminium.

Danish **SØGRENI** bicycles are more classic, but they are still outstanding in finish and design. Every one of them is individually crafted, both with numerous original details and also some very basic functions. A grey-silver colour scheme is matched with genuine leather saddles and grips add to the solid impression of quality. Søren Søgreni also produce unique flat, wooden mudguards, practical, stylish bells, lights and trouser leg clips.

Phones are another Nordic speciality. The Swedish firm **ERICSSON** has been a pioneer in designing and manufacturing phones since it was formed more than a century ago. One of its most famous models was the upright standing Ericofon (above, 1956). Today the company's Sony Ericsson division specializes in manufacturing mobile phones, such as the T68i (top right), P800 (bottom right) and T300 (far right). All models are considerably smaller than the first mobile phones of the early 1980s (below right).

The Finnish firm **NOKIA** is a leading international producer of mobile phones. Design has been an important element in the success of the Nokia phones from the late 1980s, as the company was aware from outset that mobile phones were not just high-tech equipment but personal gadgets, as important for the individual's identity as any other fashionable object. The philosophy is clearly shown in the colourful 5100 model (below). Nokia has also been quick to develop new functions, such as the wireless mobile multiplayer game deck N-gage (top).

The Danish firm **BANG & OLUFSEN** (B&O) is an internationally recognized brand, relying heavily on innovative design in their exclusive television-sets and CD-players. From the 1965 transistor radio Beolit 600 (top left) by Danish designer **JACOB JENSEN** (born 1926) to the Beosound series of the twenty-first century, which was designed by **DAVID LEWIS** (born 1939), B & O have changed the appearances of the audiovisual equipment with the times, creating lifestyle choices that are high-tech jewellery.

Hasselblad has a long running collaboration with NASA, and the cameras were used by the Apollo astronauts during their missions to the Moon in the late 1960s and early 1970s.

When the Swedish inventor **VICTOR HASSELBLAD** (1906–78) developed the first 6 x 6 reflex camera in 1948 Swedish pioneering industrial designer **SIXTEN SASON** played vital role in giving the Hasselblad camera its form. Sason minimized the camera's housing, creating it as a compact block, and succeeded in keeping the number of buttons and levers needed to an absolute minimum. The design, which was considered an ergonomic masterpiece, has been maintained.

The history of **ABLOY**, a Finnish lock manufacturer, goes back several hundred years. Since the Finnish studio **CREADESIGN** started re-thinking the design of the locks in the early 1990s, though, a distinct new era has emerged. The robust heaviness of the Abloy locks contrasts to other products by Creadesign, which are distinguished by their extreme lightness, for example the official Olympic ski pole for Exel (1988), and the feather-light collapsible chair, Trice.

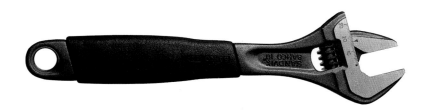

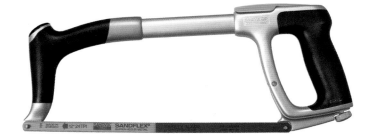

The Swedish company **BAHCO**, one of the world's largest manufacturers of saws, blades and tools has always paid great attention to ergonomics. In collaboration with Swedish **ERGONOMI DESIGN GROUP**, Bahco has developed several series of tools with extra functional and precisely studied grips. The company is deeply engaged in the prevention of work-related injuries, taking an active role in international research of the subject.

"The bricks that dreams are built of" has been said of Danish children's toy manufacturer **LEGO**. Kids play with the small multi-coloured plastic pieces all over the world. The idea for Lego originated in the 1930s, and was invented by the entrepreneurial visionary **OLE KIRK CHRISTIANSEN**. It is now one of Denmark's most design-oriented companies, always pushing forward new creative ideas. The biggest challenge in the new Millennium has been to carry the "brick-layers" into the computer era, the result of which has been the "Mindstorms" series – little plastic bricks that can do just anything.

The Finnish company **FISKARS** specializes in scissors and cutting tools, with a history dating back to the seventeenth century. In the 1950s the company asked silversmith **BERTEL GARDBERG** to design their cutlery Triennale (1957) and they took a new path. Ten years later the first pair of scissors with brightly coloured plastic grips, designed by **OLOF BÄCKSTRÖM** was unveiled to immediate success. Since then the flow of international design prizes speaks a clear language. As do the many attempts to copy these ergonomically well analysed and visually striking Finnish originals.

The wind blows almost constantly in Denmark, which led to experiments with wind turbines as far back as the 1920s. Since the oil crises and nuclear power debates of the late twentieth century the technique has drawn more and more interest. Times are good for the windmill industry, and the Danish company **VESTAS WIND SYSTEMS** is the largest manufacturer in the world. The idea behind the mills that are designed by the company, is that they have optimum features enclosed within minimal structures – a classic Scandinavian design approach.

Cast iron stoves are another Danish speciality. This stove, though, in cast iron and steel was designed by Icelandic artist **HANNES LARUSSON**. In his craft Larusson often deals with the relationships between contemporary art and the ethnic and cultural heritage, as well as with the ties between crafts and conceptualism.

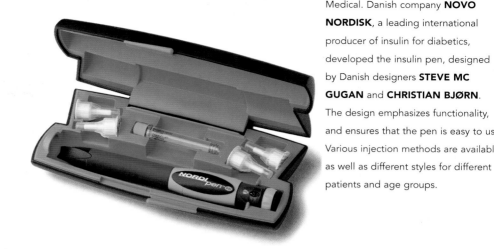

Medical. Danish company **NOVO NORDISK**, a leading international producer of insulin for diabetics, developed the insulin pen, designed by Danish designers **STEVE MC GUGAN** and **CHRISTIAN BJØRN**. The design emphasizes functionality, and ensures that the pen is easy to use. Various injection methods are available, as well as different styles for different patients and age groups.

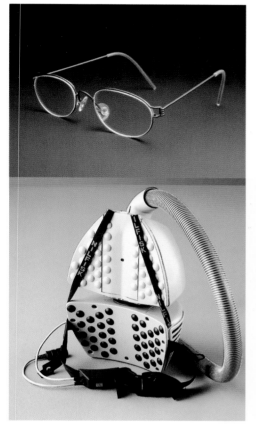

Optical. The Air Titanium spectacles, designed by Danish architects **DISSING & WEITLING** for Danish company **LINDBERG** are super-light, and free of screws, rivets and soldering. Frames are individually hand crafted, and the titanium used of a hypo-allergenic quality. The design approach is minimal, for maximum expressiveness.

Spinal. Professional cleaners often carry heavy machines on their backs. The Backuum model, designed by Danish industrial designer **STEEN MANSFELDT ERIKSEN** for **NILFISK** aimed for an ergonomically optimal solution. The motor is worn on the hip, the dust bag on the back, and the two are connected by a flexible element. The weakest part of the body carries the lightest burden.

Horizontal. The BD Relax easy chair by Swedish designer **BJÖRN DAHLSTRÖM** gives maximum comfort even in the cold. Dahlström, who has worked in the fields of graphic and industrial design as well as furniture, likes to create simple solutions with a twist of innovation. He also wants his furniture to have a profoundly graphic appearance.

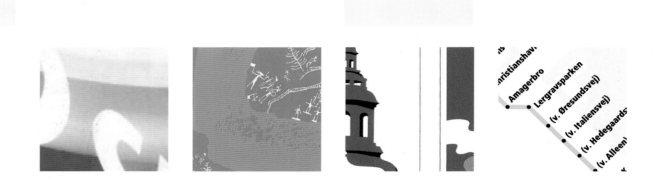

The role of graphic design in the Scandinavian new wave is as prominent as that of furniture, silver or glass. Graphics can be about wild and impressive symbols of modernity, as in the case of the Icelandic design catalogue *Mót* from the 2000 Reykjavik exhibition of the same name. This exhibition, the name of which means both mould and junction, included everything from fashion and architecture to ceramics and web design, and marked an epoch in Scandinavian graphics. The experimental leap into the future, so typical of today's Icelandic culture, was repeated in the exhibition's catalogue design, which was created by multimedia artist Dóra Ísleifsdóttir, who also works at Iceland's only multinational American advertising agency. With its maze of lines, variants of experimental typography and manipulated pictures, the catalogue was more like a web production, although on paper. "You couldn't do this in Sweden," commented an impressed reporter in a Swedish graphic design magazine. "None of the double-page spreads is in any way like the others."

Or graphic design could express something completely different, such as the corporate image of the Scandinavian airline SAS, which was produced by Stockholm Design Lab, unveiled in 1998 and went on to receive attention of the most glamorous dimensions. Here it was a case of a complete overhaul of both the inside and outside of the aircraft, and of the graphics used in every aspect of the company's image – including a subtly adjusted logo, a new house font called "Scandinavian", airport lounge fittings and the uniforms of the whole staff. This project was the total opposite of the Icelandic catalogue. The aim here was not to reflect contradictions by daringly crossing all boundaries, but to convey a sense of

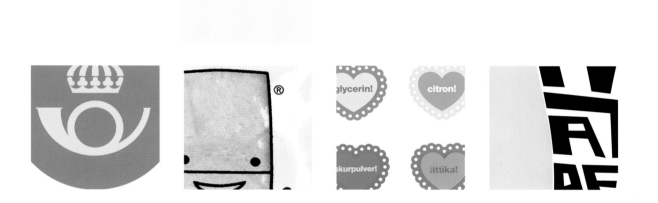

tradition and quality by employing all the well-known cool and clean lines from the received concept of Scandinavian Design. At the same time it aimed to dust off the old design clichés, to modernize and update them. The message "It's Scandinavian" is also repeated a mantra in the new, improved image of the airline.

However different these examples may appear to be, they both show that graphics are in the same league as the other design genres. This wasn't the case in the 1950s. One or two harmonically clear fonts may have seen the light of day such as the well-known Berlings antique, which was drawn by Karl-Erik Forsberg in 1955. The prevailing ideal of the time was also reflected in book and magazine design. But, unlike other genres, graphic design did not work to the same degree as an end in itself, rather it stood as an attuned design background for the more definite three-dimensional achievements. One difference is probably connected to the fact that the media of the time had not been turned into the "message", in other words, the field of communication did not play the same dominant role that it does today.

Delightful – that is to say both attractive and effective – contemporary book and magazine design is an evident feature of the design culture of the Nordic countries, a tradition that was first extended to media such as TV and the Internet during the 1990s. This is particularly true when it comes to the design of the daily papers – countries such as Denmark and Sweden have put their best foot forward in an international context, bringing home prizes and honourable mentions by the dozen in the annual competition of the trade organization Society for News Design (SND). The Nordic daily press often distinguishes itself with

its attractive and reader-friendly design, which is by no means extreme but still pleasing. Two leading daily newspapers in particular, Denmark's *Politiken* and Sweden's *Dagens Nyheter*, have attracted considerable attention at awards ceremonies for their pure graphic presentation, the construction and layout of the papers' pages, photography and illustrations. The Danes have especially excelled in the field of photojournalism. Both newspapers have been responsible for many awards in the prestigious World Press Photo competition and, photographers such as Joachim Ladefoged, have broken into the legendary photographic agency Magnum.

Sweden has instead fostered a large number of impressive illustrators. Fashion illustrator Mats Gustafson, now resident in New York and among the world's design elite, paved the way in the 1970s and 1980s with his economical but at the same time characterful and expressive pictures, primarily in flowing watercolours and pastel crayons. Today lively, stylistic illustrations by Nordic illustrators are almost the rule in magazines such as *Wallpaper*. Just as in the 1990s, Nordic fashion photographers are often seen in leading international fashion magazines and Scandinavian art directors have been responsible for designing a large number of cosmopolitan publications from *Blueprint* to *Harper's Bazaar*.

Another field in which Scandinavians have made an international impact is cartoons. For many years Sweden has published considerable numbers of cartoon strips and had a lively alternative culture, which is rooted in the successful comic publisher Galago. Through programmes such as Magnus Carlsson's animated TV series *Robin and the Three Friends … and Jerry*, Swedish cartoon culture has had major international hits. The latter series, for example, was shown on one of America's major channels every day

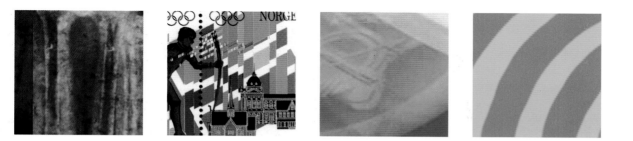

for a year. Finnish alternative series have also made a reputation for themselves, while their Danish counterparts have concentrated on the comical adventure tradition *à la* Tintin. Teddy Kristiansen, however, achieved instant international fame when he became the first non-American behind an official Superman book (*Superman and the Tale of Five Cities*). Furthermore the Norwegians have caught up recently with successes like Frode Øverli's daily strip *Pondus*, which sold to many countries in Europe, and with the small publisher Jippi, which is home to artistic stars such as series creator John Arne Sätteröy, known as Jason.

The more business-oriented, corporate identity graphics – apart from SAS – are dominated to a great degree by well-known brands of beer and spirits such as Carlsberg, Tuborg and Absolut, which have succeeded in keeping the Scandinavian flag flying throughout the world. On the other hand ambitious efforts on the domestic plane have been for the public services. Even milk has been the source of inspiration in several of the Nordic countries with fresh and spiritual packaging. In Denmark and Sweden, however, the Post Offices have been among the greatest graphic challenges. In both cases leading brand experts were called in to create new profiles for the new millennium, to clarify and modernize the traditional postal services. In both cases the results were controversial. The Danish Post Office's cheerful red visual identity introduced from 1993–98 by Danish Kontrapunkt in association with Studio Dumbar from the Netherlands is seen by the critics as being too colourful and having connotations with an amusement park. Meanwhile, in Sweden the overriding yellow graphic design, revealed in 2001 by the Swedish firm Formula DDB, was viewed as being so internationally acceptable as to be almost bland.

The visual identity of the Danish Post Office, which has traditionally been cast in red and white to resemble the Danish flag, received a new look in the late 1990s, designed by **KIM MEYER ANDERNSEN** and **BO LINNEMAN** of visual identity consultants **KONTRAPUNKT**. The blue, green and yellows of the logo are intended to symbolize the new, independent status of the Post Office, which incorporates several new fields of operation.

Stamps from the Nordic countries give a visual hint of the cultural values of the region, and Post Office logos from Norway (left) and Sweden (right), the latter redesigned for the twenty-first century by **PETER NEUMEISTER** from visual identity studio **FORMULA DDB**.

Young boys reflected in the windscreen of a parked car play in the street of Sanaa, Yemen. Scandinavian photojournalism has high standards. Danish photographers in particular have repeatedly received prominent awards in international competitions such as World Press Photo. In 2002 this picture won Danish photographer **JOACHIM LADEFOGED**, a member of Magnum and on assignment for *Geo* magazine, a prize in the "Daily Life" category of the competition.

Visual identity: airport.
The Billund Airport brand,
designed by Danish design
consultants **KONTRAPUNKT**,
uses the contrasting colours
yellow and grey. The design
programme encompassed
a new name and set of core
elements: logotype, corporate
typeface and colours.
The Billund "Bee", a
communicative fifth element,
which represents the name of
the airport.

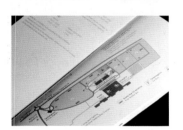

Visual identity: finance. The corporate branding programme for the Danish bank, Danske Bank, which was also designed by
KONTRAPUNKT, is business-like and cool. The design program, for which Kontrapunkt was awarded the Danish Design Prize in
2001, encompassed a logo, a new corporate typeface and a environmentally friendly signs.

Green is the identifying colour of **CARLSBERG**, the Danish beer manufacturer, which is internationally known for the legend "probably the best lager in the world". The green theme has lingered in Carlsberg's advertising campaigns over the years.

The **ABSOLUT** campaign story started with an advertisement bearing the words "Absolut Perfection" in 1980. When **ANDY WARHOL** did his Absolut Vodka bottle painting in 1985 the unconventional "Absolut Art" ad concept was born. Since then around five hundred artists, photographers, fashion designers and art directors have "interpreted" the famous Swedish medicine bottle. Meanwhile the **FINLANDIA** bottle, has an equally recognizable identity.

Event graphics: Winter Olympics. When in 1994 the Norwegians had the honour of hosting the winter games in Lillehammer all efforts were gathered to create a high quality visual profile, with a strong emphasis on Norway's distinctive features, traditions and national character. Diversity, vigour and joy should be the ideals of the games, which are elements that are visible in all these graphics.

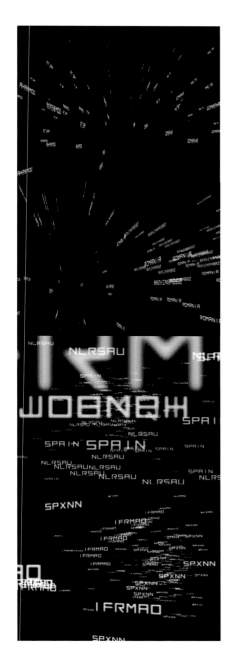

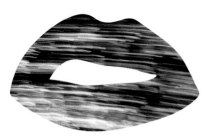

EUROVISION SONG CONTEST
STOCKHOLM 2000

Event graphics: Eurovision Song Contest. In 1998 this television show, which is watched by millions all over Europe, was hosted in Stockholm, the appealing graphics, which created a strong visual identity, were designed by Swedish agency **STOCKHOLM DESIGN LAB**, where graphic designer **BJÖRN KUSOFFSKY** is co-founder and head of visual designs (above).

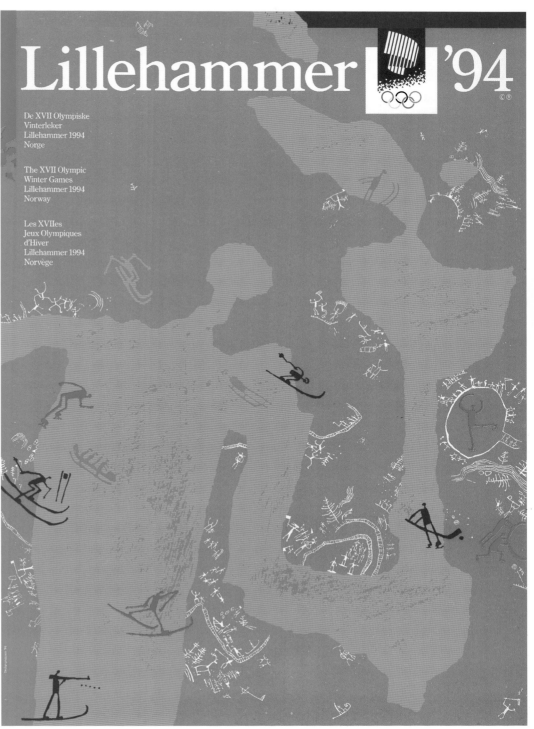

Lillehammer '94

De XVII Olympiske
Vinterleker
Lillehammer 1994
Norge

The XVII Olympic
Winter Games
Lillehammer 1994
Norway

Les XVIIes
Jeux Olympiques
d'Hiver
Lillehammer 1994
Norvège

Scandinavian signage: anonymous. The road signs of the northern countries hardly could be accused of graphic refinement. But they still have their own exotic grandeur, simply because of the motifs of the signs, which foreign tourists steal as holiday souvenirs. Where else do you find road signs with elk, skiers and snow scooters?

Scandinavian signage: high profile. Transport systems have always offered glorious work for graphic designers, ever since Johnston & Beck developed the typeface and map for the London tube. The twenty-first century Metro in Copenhagen is no exception. Respected Danish designer **PER MOLLERUP** of Mollerup Designlab won the competition to design the graphic programme for the Copenhagen underground. The typeface chosen for the programme was Frutiger 77 black condensed. As a Danish "ø" was added to it, the typeface was given the honorary title "metro sign face".

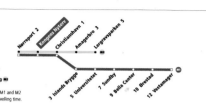

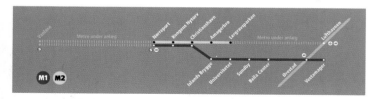

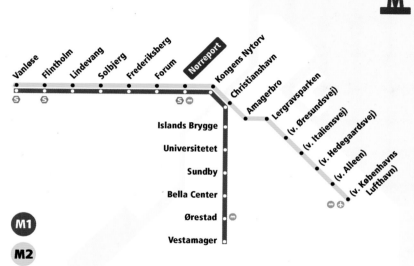

The **BERLINGS ANTIKVA**
typeface, which was designed
by Swedish graphic artist **KARL-
ERIK FORSBERG** (1914–95) was
the typical font of Scandinavian
Design in the golden days of
the 1950s (right).

BerlingEF-Regular Typeface
BerlingEF-Italic Typeface
BerlingEF-Bold Typeface

The Swedish design collective **ACNE** works with graphics as well as film and fashion (see p.167). For Scandinavian Airlines (SAS) Acne designed quirky little symbols to decorate the airline's special packaging for children's items such as such as ketchup and cookies. The clean and rational SAS corporate identity ,including the sub-logo "Its Scandinavian", was designed by the Swedish design agency Stockholm Design Lab.

The man behind *Robin and the Three friends … and Jerry* (left) and *Nils Ossian Uniformed* (below) is the acclaimed Swedish cartoonist **MAGNUS CARLSSON**. He has several international successes such as *Robin and Da Mob* to his credit, and his animations have been aired all over the world.

© 1999 Magnus Carlsson, Happylife Animation AB, TV-Loonland AG

The striking, colourful illustrations by Swedish graphic artist **LOTTA KÜHLHORN** have been frequently displayed in international media such as *Wallpaper* magazine. Her style is at once lucid and cute.

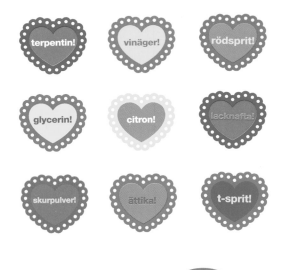

Marcel Beyer
Spioner

Panache
Albert Bonniers Förlag

Jenny Erpenbeck
Smäck

Panache
Albert Bonniers Förlag

Michel Houellebecq
Plattform

Panache
Albert Bonniers Förlag

Amin Zaoui
Kvinnoväktarna

Panache
Albert Bonniers Förlag

LOTTA KÜHLHORN also
works as a graphic designer
of books, combing a sense
for a colourful and visual
narrative with knowledge
and understanding of functional,
easy-to-read typography.

Hungarian-born graphic designer **GABOR PALOTAI**, who lives and works in Sweden, is renowned for powerful imagery, using the simplest of elements and structures. In his book *Maximizing the Audience*, which he published himself, he organizes his work under titles like "Dimensions", "Textures", "Numbers", "Elements" and "Death". The projects he covers include signage, interactive media, corporate identity, handmade carpets, illustration and photography.

Swedish graphic designer **LARS SUNDH** is one of the founders of the Modernista Publishing House, having previously run urban magazines such as *Pop* and *Bibel*. The independent Modernista publishes around 35 titles a year, the visual appearance of the books overseen by Sundh. For Modernista's series of paperback classics he designed the Chernobyl typeface.

The portfolio of Danish graphic designer studio **2GD**, which consists of designers **JAN NIELSEN** and **OLE LUND**, includes prestigious international customers such as Carlsberg, Coca Cola, the Danish Broadcasting Corporation and Sony Nordic. Still the two designers give priority to independence and innovation, concentrating on always taking things one step further. Earthly irony and abstract constructivism are indicative of the studio's special creative formula.

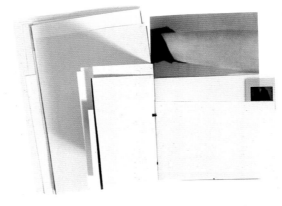

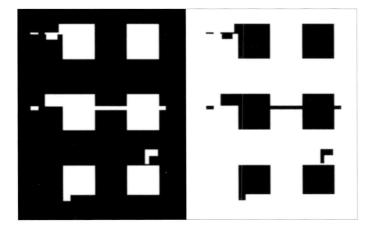

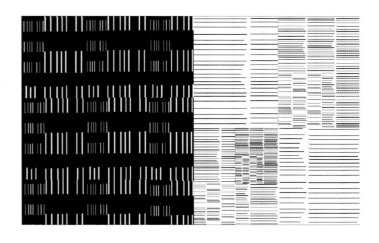

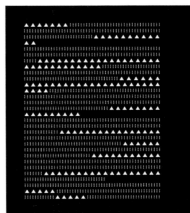

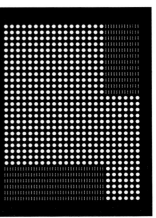

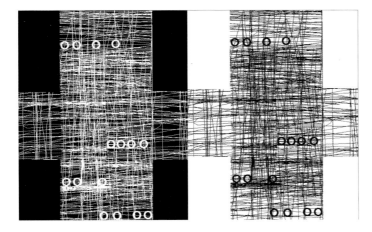

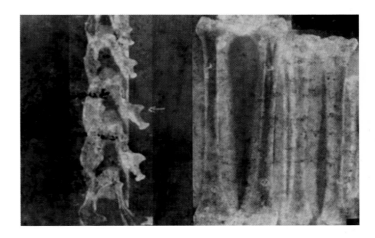

INDEX

PICTURE CREDITS

The publishers would like to thank the following
sources for their kind permission to reproduce
the pictures in this book:

Abloy Security Ltd.: 200
Absolut: 214bl
Acne: 167, 217m
Adelta: 100br, 100tr
Åke E:son Lindman: 18, 19, 26, 27br, 27tl, 27tr,
28, 30t, 31, 37, 115, 116, 118,122, 123b, 123t,
124-125, 126b, 126t, 127, 132, 135
Alvar Aalto Museum: 22b, 22tr, 23b, 23t, 120tl,
120tr
Anders Amlo: 12b
Andreas Engesvik Design AS: 106bl
Anna Holtblad AB: 160
Arabia Oy: 57b, 57t, 70bl, 73
Arcaid: Richard Bryant:115
Arne-Jacobsen.com: Strüwing: 20t, 20b, 21b, 21t;
/ 90t, 90b, 100tl
Artek: 88bl, 88br, 88m, 88tr, 89
Arvesund: 86mr, 87tl, 87tr
Asplund: 83, 87b, 98br, 99b, 99tl, 99tr
Bang & Olufsen: 198
Bildhuset AB: Åke E:son Lindman: 176bm; /Bengt
Olof Olsson: 179t, 187bl; /Björn Keller: 180ml,
184bl; /Björn Lindberg: 177t, 179bl, 179br, 180m,
182tl;/Pelle Bergström: 180br, 180mr,180mt;/Per
Klaesson: 176br;/Robert Blomback: 180tr; /Stellan
Herner:176m;/Torbjörn Boström: 180bm;/179tr
Biomega: 195
Bjorn Borg: 166bl
Bruno Mathsson International AB: 82br
Bruuns Bazaar A/S: 169
Carl Malmsten: 82bl
Carlsberg: 214
Cbi: 96b, 96t
Cecilia Johansson: 152m
Cherrox: 167
Claesson-Koivisto-Rune: Patrik Engquist: 124, 134;
/ 95
Corbis: Carmen Redondo: 10t; /Kevin Schafer: 13tl;
/ 216cl, 216cr, 216tl, 216tr, 216tcr
Daughters of Style: 168
Danish Design Center: 62t, 70tl, 112b, 112t
Danish Post Office: 210
Dansk Møbelkunst: 50l
David Design: 103t, 105bl
Design House Stockholm: 61
Dissing+Weitling arkitektfirma a/s: 205tl
Entasis: Peter Lind Bonderup: 36b, 36t
Ergonomi Design: 58mb, 58t, 58m, 201
Eva Denmark: 64b, 64tl, 64tr, 65tr
Fennopress: Paavo Martikainen: 132; /178b;
/Sakari Parkkinen: 184t
Figgio: 66
Finlandia Vodka: 214bm
Filippa K AB: 162ml
Fjällräven AB: 170b
Föreningen Stockholms Företagsminnen: 196bl,
196tl
Formgivare Henrik Nygren AB: 9br
Fiskars Consumer Oy Ab: 203
Fredericia: 82t, 86b
Fritz Hansen A/S: Thomas Ibsen: 94b
Furniture Factory Korhonen: 82bc
Gabor Palotai: 221
Garsnas AB: 102b, 103b
Georg Jensen: 52
Günther Flake GbR: 217tm
Hackman: 11b, 72, 76
Hannes Lárusson: 204br
Heikkinen-Komonen Architects: Jussi Tiainen:
39b, 39t
Helen & Hard AS: 107b
Helena Lehtinen: 148ml, 148mr, 148tl, 148tr
Helene Toresdotter: 177bl, 177br, 178tl, 178tr,
179mr, 180bl, 180bm, 181, 182b, 182tm, 183br,
183m, 184bm, 184br, 185, 186, 187t
Hilde Dramstad: 152t
Hulton Archive: 192b
Iceland Post: 211
Iform: 84b, 84t, 85
Inger Marie Berg: 152b
Iittala: Markku Alatolo: 53; / 48b, 49, 56c, 75
Inno Avarte: 100bl
Janicke Horn: 144b, 144t
Jarmund/Vigsnaes: 41
Jasper Saalto: 94b
Jesper Persson: 70tr
Jiri Havran: 40, 121
J Lindberg: 163
Jonas Lindvall: 1, 86t, 129
Kallemo: 92
Kay Bojesen: 56bc

Kirsten Clausager: 153mr
Komplot: 107m
Kontrapunkt: 213
Kvadrat: 67
L'Agence VU: Joachim Ladefoged: 212
Lammhults: 93tl, 97, 98tl, 104b, 104t
Lervik: 106bc
Lotta Kühlhorn: 218, 219
Mads Nørgaard: 164
Magnus Carlsson: 217b, 217br
Marimekko: Klikki: 54b, 54t, 77, 155
Martela: 93cl
Modernista: 220tl
Mollerup-Design Lab: 216bl, 216br, 216cl
Munthe Plus Simonsen: 165
Museum of Finnish Architecture: 113, 120b
National Museum, Stockholm: 65l
News Design DFE AB: 106bml, 106br
Nilfisk: 205ml
Nokia Mobile Phone Communications: 196br, 197
Novo Nordisk: 205tr
Olympic Museum Collections: 215m, 215tm
One Little Indian: 13br
Offecct: 105cr
Orrefors Kosta Boda: Michael Forster: 51b, 51t;
/Per Larsson: 50c; /Pelle Wahlgren: 50r; /
71;/Roland Persson: 74
Päivi Kekäläinen: 48t
Peder Musse: 146b, 146t
Per Spook: 158
Pernille Klemp: 147, 150ml, 151, 153b, 153mr,
153tr
Per Suntum: 150t, 150b
Pia Wallén Design AB: 153tl, 161
Piiroinen: 91, 102bl
Post Norway: 211, 211tr
Post Sweden: 211tr
Pritzker Architecture Prize: 41b
Reima: 170t
Rex Features: IBL: 176bl, 176tl;/Lehitikuva Oy: 11t,
40, 114;/ 183tl, 184bm
Royal Copenhagen: 60
Rukka: 170m
Saab: 193
Saldo: 59bl, 59br, 59tl, 59tr
Sanna Hansson: 105t
Schmidt, Hammer & Lassen: 94t
Science Photo Library: Volker Steger: 202
Skeepshult: 205b
Snohetta AS: 12tr
Snowcrash: 106bc, 106t,
Sögreni of Copenhagen: 194
Sony Ericsson Mobile Communications AB: 196m
Søren Kuhn: 30b, 33b, 33t, 133b, 133tr
Søren Robert Lund Arkitekter: 35
Stelton A/S: 62-63
Stockholm Design Lab: 215tl, 215bl
Stokke: 102cl,102tl
Studio Ilkka Suppanen: 107t
Synnøve Korssjøen: 148b, 148m
Tiger: 162tr
Tone Vigeland: Guri Dahl:142, 143
Tore Svensson: 145
VA Arkitektar: Ragnar Th /www.arctic-images.com:
42b, 42t, 43
Verner Panton Design: 101b, 101t, 113
Vestas Wind Systems A/S: 204t
Vibeke Rohland: 10br, 68, 69
Victor Hasselblad AB: 199
View Pictures: Dennis Gilbert: 32br, 32t, 130,
131b, 131t
Volvo Car Corporation: 192tl
Whyred: 166tr
Wingårdh Arkitektkontor AB: Ulf Celander: 29
Woodnotes: 55bc, 55tr, 137
2GD/2GRAPHICDESIGN A/S: 220b
3XNielsen A/S: Adam Mork: 36b; /Finn
Christoffersen: 36tl

Every effort has been made to acknowledge
correctly and contact the source and/or copyright
holder of each picture, and Carlton Books Limited
apologises for any unintentional errors, or
omissions, which will be corrected in future editions
of this book.